do-it-yourself do-it-yourself
do-it-yourself do-it-yourself
do-it-yourself do-it-yourself
do-it-yourself do-it-yourself
do-it-yourself do-it-yourself
do-it-yourself do-it-yourself
do-it-yourself do-it-yourself
do-it-yourself do-it-yourself
do-it-yourself do-it-yourself
do-it-yourself do-it-yourself
do-it-yourself do-it-yourself
do-it-yourself do-it-yourself
do-it-yourself do-it-yourself
do-it-yourself do-it-yourself
do-it-yourself do-it-yourself
do-it-yourself do-it-yourself
do-it-yourself do-it-yourself
do-it-yourself do-it-yourself
do-it-yourself do-it-yourself
do-it-yourself do-it-yourself
do-it-yourself do-it-yourself
do-it-yourself do-it-yourself
do-it-yourself do-it-yourself
do-it-yourself do-it-yourself
do-it-yourself do-it-yourself
do-it-yourself do-it-yourself
do-it-yourself do-it-yourself
do-it-yourself do-it-yourself
do-it-yourself do-it-yourself
do-it-yourself do-it-yourself
do-it-yourself do-it-yourself
do-it-yourself do-it-yourself
do-it-yourself do-it-yourself
do-it-yourself do-it-yourself
do-it-yourself do-it-yourself
do-it-yourself do-it-yourself
do-it-yourself do-it-yourself
do-it-yourself do-it-yourself
do-it-yourself do-it-yourself
do-it-yourself do-it-yourself
do-it-yourself do-it-yourself
do-it-yourself do-it-yourself
do-it-yourself do-it-yourself

HOME
COMFORT

do-it-yourself do-it-yourself
do-it-yourself do-it-yourself
do-it-yourself do-it-yourself
do-it-yourself do-it-yourself
do-it-yourself do-it-yourself
do-it-yourself do-it-yourself
do-it-yourself do-it-yourself
do-it-yourself do-it-yourself
do-it-yourself do-it-yourself
do-it-yourself do-it-yourself
do-it-yourself do-it-yourself
do-it-yourself do-it-yourself
do-it-yourself do-it-yourself
do-it-yourself do-it-yourself
do-it-yourself do-it-yourself
do-it-yourself do-it-yourself
do-it-yourself do-it-yourself
do-it-yourself do-it-yourself
do-it-yourself do-it-yourself
do-it-yourself do-it-yourself
do-it-yourself do-it-yourself
do-it-yourself do-it-yourself
do-it-yourself do-it-yourself
do-it-yourself do-it-yourself
do-it-yourself do-it-yourself
do-it-yourself do-it-yourself
do-it-yourself do-it-yourself
do-it-yourself do-it-yourself
do-it-yourself do-it-yourself
do-it-yourself do-it-yourself
do-it-yourself do-it-yourself
do-it-yourself do-it-yourself
do-it-yourself do-it-yourself
do-it-yourself do-it-yourself
do-it-yourself do-it-yourself
do-it-yourself do-it-yourself

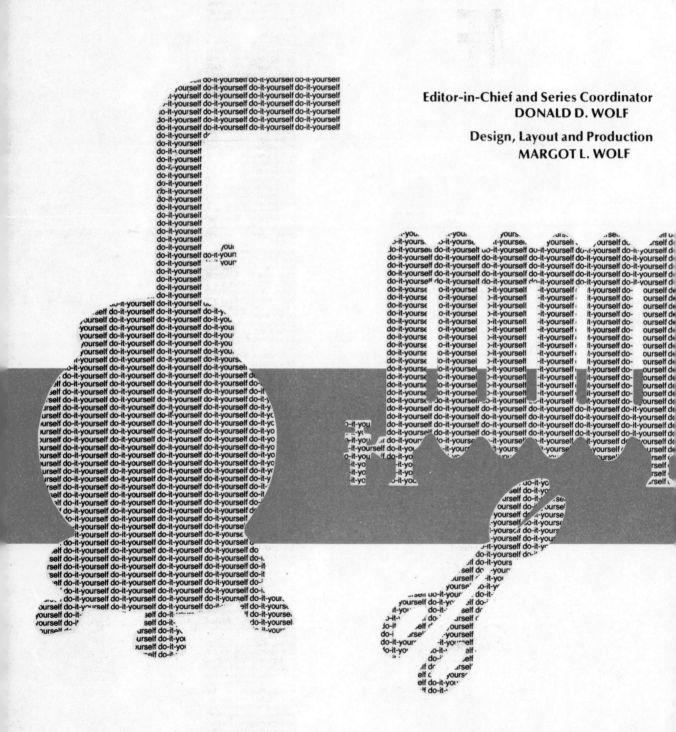

Editor-in-Chief and Series Coordinator
DONALD D. WOLF

Design, Layout and Production
MARGOT L. WOLF

ADVENTURES IN HOME REPAIR SERIES

HOME COMFORT

Written by
DICK DEMSKE

Illustrated by
JAMES E. BARRY

Consolidated Book Publishers
NEW YORK • CHICAGO

Introduction

It wasn't too long ago—well within the memory of many of us—that home comfort conditioning meant a wood- or coal-burning stove in winter and a hand-held fan in summer. Obviously, times have changed for the better, much better. Today, just about every house (except for some backwoods retreats and, alas, some decaying tenements) is equipped with some form of central heating system. And, more and more, the summer heat is being conquered through air conditioning. Over the past several years, the cost of room air conditioners has dropped dramatically to the point at which they are within reach of almost any sweating suburbanite or uncomfortable urbanite. About the only restriction on summertime indoor comfort now is the sometimes-flawed ability of the power company to deliver the "juice" when it's needed the most. The very fact that peak power requirements now occur on the hottest summer days, rather than during the winter evenings as was the case just a few years back, attests to the overwhelming popularity of air conditioning.

Prices may have come down, but an air conditioner or a heating unit represents a major investment. You should be well informed before you make it, and once you have laid out your hard-earned dollars (aren't they all hard-earned?) you should treat that investment well, giving it the proper maintenance and keeping it in tune. With costs of all fuels likely to keep spiraling upward, this is more important than ever if you are to enjoy year-round indoor comfort.

There is much you can do yourself to insure comfort at a cost you can afford; other installation, maintenance, and repair chores should be attempted only by skilled amateurs or left to the professionals. To help you make this decision, we have graded the how-to projects in this book according to degree of difficulty, as determined by consultations with professional heating engineers and contractors as well as home handymen. Projects deemed within the capabilities of the novice do-it-yourselfer are marked ● . Those that might be attempted by more skilled persons are marked ▲ . More difficult projects, which should be attempted by only the most accomplished do-it-yourselfers or left to the professionals, are marked ■ . Of course, you must be the final judge of your competence in these fields. If you think you can do it, good luck! But don't get in over your head.

Every effort has been made to ensure the accuracy, reliability, and currentness of the information and instructions in this book. But changes are constantly taking place in the heating and air-conditioning industry. And we are not infallible. Neither are you. We cannot guarantee that there are no omissions, no human or typographical errors herein, nor can we guarantee that you will not err in following our directions. If that happens, we only hope that it will not discomfort you too much nor for too long. Keep cool—and warm!

DONALD D. WOLF

Library of Congress Catalog Card Number: 76-52269
International Standard Book Number: 0-8326-2217-6

Contents

1

Heating Systems

THE HEATING SYSTEM is something of a mystery to most homeowners. Of course, they are painfully aware of it when they groan over the monthly fuel bills, and even more so when they awaken on the coldest morning of the year to discover that the furnace went to sleep right after they did and the thermostat has frosted over. But beyond that, it's just a maze of pipes coming out of a strange box in the basement or the utility room. A necessary evil – and just hope that it keeps on cooking!

It needn't be that way. We certainly don't recommend that the average do-it-yourselfer should design and install his own heating system. That is very definitely a job for the reputable professional contractor or the most knowledgeable and experienced amateur. The professional should also be called on to inspect the system annually. But there are many things that you can do to help your heating system operate more dependably, more efficiently, and more economically. And before you can do that, you must first understand just how it operates.

It seems likely that man has been conscious of his cold-weather comfort ever since he started fooling around with fire (probably quite accidentally) untold millennia ago. That wondrous discovery led to "space heaters" on the floors of caves and later in pits dug into the earthen floors of crude huts and in braziers in the homes and palaces of kings, pharaohs, and the just plain wealthy and powerful. Sometime around the first century A.D., the Romans conceived the idea of central heating, building subterranean fires to warm floors and, hopefully, the rooms above. At about the same time, the Chinese invented a system by which heat from central ovens was directed through pipes to the various rooms of a dwelling. Sound familiar?

Surprisingly, the idea of central heating was slow to gain widespread acceptance – about 1,900 years. Although increasingly sophisticated central-heating equipment has been installed in most American homes built over the past 50 years or so, the idea is only now catching on in many other parts of the world, including Europe, Australia, southern Africa – and China, where it all began!

But we don't mean to put down space heating. It is a perfectly good concept and has a very important place as supplementary heating and in such installations as homes in very warm climates (where it may be needed only to "take off the chill" on some of the cooler nights), and summer cottages and ski chalets that are not intended as full-time residences.

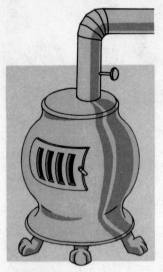

Pot-bellied stove.

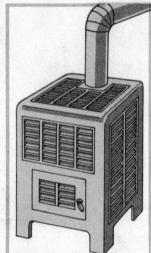

Circulator heater.

Grilles in doors and walls
to allow circulation of air.

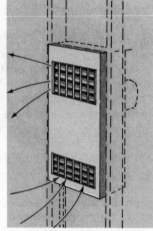

Vertical wall heater.

SPACE HEATING UNITS

Space heaters, also called area heaters, are installed in the room or area to be heated. They include stoves, circulator heaters, and "pipeless" heaters.

Stoves are one of the simplest heating devices and also among the dirtiest (after the open fire). They also require more attention and heat less uniformly than most others. But they are relatively inexpensive. Most of them burn wood or coal and heat by radiation. If more than one stove is used, more than one chimney may be needed. Stoves are suitable for a backwoods hunting lodge or similar installation; otherwise, they are not very satisfactory.

Circulator heaters heat by convection, passing heat from an outer jacket. They are available for burning wood, coal, oil, or gas. With proper arrangement of rooms and doors, a circulator heater can heat four or five small rooms, but the heating may not be uniform. A small fan to aid circulation will increase efficiency. The distance from the heater to the center of each room to be heated, measured through the door opening, should not be more than about 18 feet. Doors must be left open, or grilles or louvers provided at top and bottom of doors or walls to allow circulation of air.

Pipeless furnaces can provide adequate

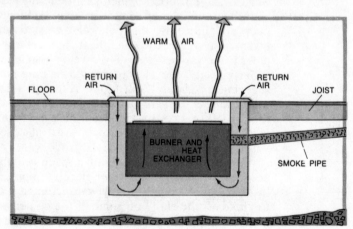

Diagram shows the working
of a floor heater.

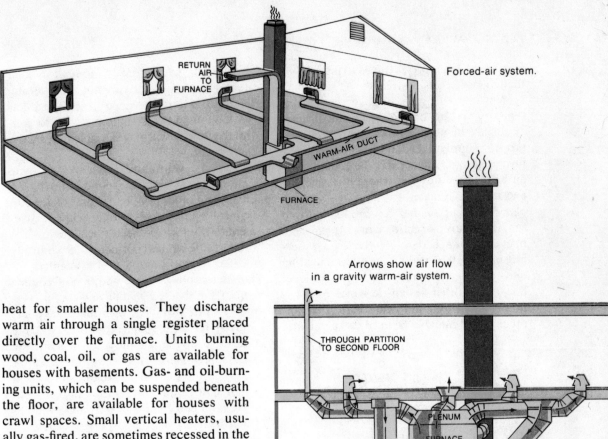

Forced-air system.

RETURN AIR TO FURNACE

WARM-AIR DUCT

FURNACE

Arrows show air flow in a gravity warm-air system.

THROUGH PARTITION TO SECOND FLOOR

PLENUM

FURNACE

heat for smaller houses. They discharge warm air through a single register placed directly over the furnace. Units burning wood, coal, oil, or gas are available for houses with basements. Gas- and oil-burning units, which can be suspended beneath the floor, are available for houses with crawl spaces. Small vertical heaters, usually gas-fired, are sometimes recessed in the walls. Such units may be either manually or thermostatically controlled. Heater vents are exhausted through the walls or carried up through the partitions to discharge burned gases through a common vent extending through the roof. Such a unit is often the choice for an extension built onto a house where the existing heating system is not up to carrying the additional load.

CENTRAL HEATING: WARM AIR

Gravity warm-air heating is typified by the big round furnace in the middle of the basement with an octupus-like network of large pipes to carry heat to the various rooms of the house. It works on the principle that warm air rises and cold air settles. Cold-air return grilles strategically located at such points as the bases of stairways and beneath large window areas collect the cool air and duct it to the bottom of the furnace. It then passes through the heating chamber into the plenum above, where it is directed through the pipes to the various room registers located in floors or baseboards.

Gravity warm-air heating systems kept many generations of Americans in comparative cold-weather comfort. But they were inefficient, sometimes erratic, and often dirty; and the low-hanging pipes, which had to be pitched upward toward the heat outlets, virtually proscribed the use of the basement for anything other than doing the laundry at the stationary tubs and similar chores. Today, gravity warm-air systems are rarely installed, although they are still found in many homes built up to 20 or so years ago.

Forced warm-air systems are more efficient and generally cost less to install than their gravity counterparts. A forced-air system consists of a furnace, ducts, and registers. A fan or blower in the furnace circulates the warm air to the various rooms through supply ducts and heat outlets. Return grilles and ducts carry the cooled room air back to the furnace, where it is reheated and then recirculated.

A forced-air system can be divided into several different sections or zones, each operating independently with its own thermostat and all served by the central heating unit. Zones are often used in split-level houses and other designs in which one section is likely to retain heat longer than another. They can also be used to keep living areas warm while conserving heat in such areas as bedrooms that are not in use during the day. Dampers placed inside the ductwork open and close automatically to control the flow of warm air as called for by the thermostat.

Forced warm-air systems provide uniform heat and respond rapidly to changes in outdoor temperatures. They can be installed in houses with or without basements—the furnace need not be below the rooms to be heated, nor need it be centrally located. Some units can be adapted for summer cooling by the addition of cooling coils. Combination heating and cooling systems can be installed, with the same ducts utilized for year-round comfort. And the ducts are up out of the way beneath the joists, allowing the basement to be used for other purposes. This development was a major spur to the proliferation of basement recreation and rumpus rooms and even extra bedrooms over the past few decades.

The warm air is usually filtered through inexpensive replaceable or washable filters. Electronic air cleaners can sometimes be installed in existing forced-air systems and are available on many furnaces for new installations. These remove pollen, fine dust, and other irritants that pass through ordinary filters and are especially helpful for persons with respiratory ailments. The more expensive units feature automatic washing and drying of the cleaner.

A humidifier may be added to the heating system to add moisture to the house air and avoid the discomfort and other disadvantages of a too-dry environment.

Warm-air supply outlets are best placed along outside walls: by heating these naturally colder areas, they are more likely to keep a uniform temperature throughout the entire room. The outlets should be low in the wall, preferably in the baseboard, where air cannot blow directly on the room's occupants. Floor registers tend to collect dust

OPEN DAMPER

CLOSED DAMPER

Diagram of air flow in zoned forced-air system.

PLENUM

FURNACE

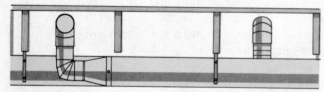

Location of ducts, run beneath joists, for a forced warm-air system.

Air filter.

Baseboard outlet.

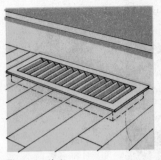

Floor outlet.

High wall outlet.

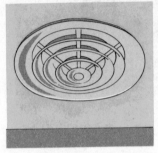

Ceiling diffuser.

Baseboard return.

Floor return.

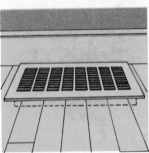
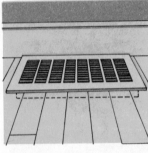

Location of return grille in cold-air trap.

and debris, but they may have to be used when installing a new system in an old house.

High wall or ceiling outlets are sometimes used when the system is designed primarily for cooling. However, satisfactory cooling as well as heating can be obtained with low wall or baseboard outlets by increasing the air volume and velocity and by properly directing the flow by adjusting register fins or louvers.

Ceiling diffusers that discharge air downward may cause drafts; those that discharge air across the ceiling may cause smudging. However, these may be the only choices in a finished basement room that is heated by the main furnace.

Most installations have a cold-air return in each room except for smaller areas such as bathrooms. When supply outlets are along outside walls, return grilles should be along inside partitions in the baseboard or floor. When supply outlets are along inside walls, as was customary with earlier forced-air systems, return grilles should be along outside walls.

Smaller homes with perimeter-type heating systems (outlets on outside walls) may have just a single, centrally located return. In two-level or split-level homes, return grilles should be on each level. Returns should be situated in natural cold-air traps, such as hallways and at the bottoms of stairways.

In houses with crawl spaces instead of basements, horizontal oil- or gas-burning

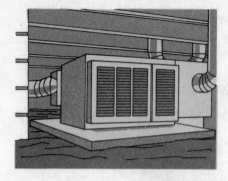

Horizontal furnace installation in crawl space.

Horizontal furnace installation in attic.

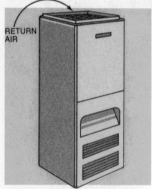

RETURN AIR

Counterflow furnace.

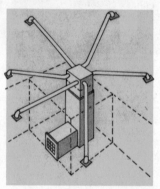

Upflow-type vertical furnace.

furnaces may be installed in the crawl space or suspended from ceiling joists in a utility room or attached garage. A gas unit of this type can also be installed in an attic. Adequate space should be allowed for servicing furnaces in crawl spaces or attics, and furnaces and ducts installed in attics should be heavily insulated to prevent excessive heat loss in these naturally cold areas.

The entire crawl space is sometimes used as an air supply plenum or chamber. Warm air from an upright furnace or a suspended horizontal furnace is forced through a central duct into the crawl space, from where it enters the rooms above through perimeter outlets, or through a series of slots in the floor adjacent to the outside walls. With tight, well-insulated crawl space walls, this system can provide comfortable, uniform temperatures throughout the house.

Vertical oil or gas furnaces designed for installation in a closet or wall recess are popular for smaller houses. A counterflow type discharges the warm air at the bottom to warm the floor level. Some types provide discharge grilles into several rooms from a centrally located furnace. Upflow-type vertical furnaces may discharge the warm air through attic ducts and ceiling diffusers. Return air is usually pulled directly into the furnace from a wall grille, rather than through return ducts. Because of this, these furnaces are less expensive, but also heat less evenly.

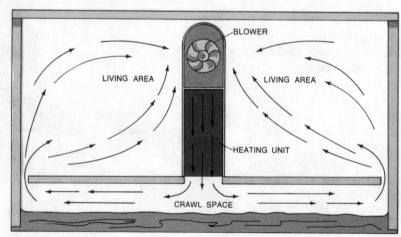

Crawl space plenum system (arrows show flow of warm air)

BLOWER

LIVING AREA

LIVING AREA

HEATING UNIT

CRAWL SPACE

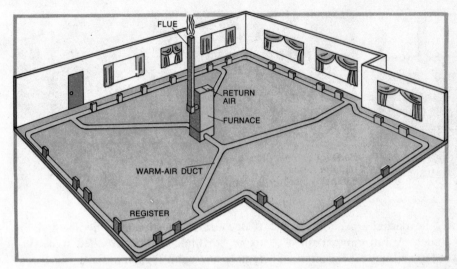

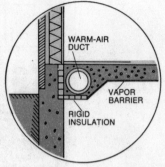

Perimeter loop system.

Houses built on concrete slabs may be heated by a "perimeter loop." A counterflow furnace circulates warm air through ducts cast around the outer edge of the slab. The warm ducts heat the floor, and the warm air is discharged through floor registers to heat the various rooms. To prevent excessive heat loss in such a system, the edge of the slab should be insulated from the outer walls and separated from the ground by a vapor barrier.

CENTRAL HEATING: HOT WATER, STEAM

Hot-water and steam heating systems are similar. Each consists of a boiler, pipes, and room-heating units (radiators or convectors). Hot water or steam, generated in the boiler, is circulated through the pipes to the room units, where the heat is transferred to the room air.

Boilers are made of cast iron or steel and are designed to burn gas, oil, or coal (which may yet make a comeback). Cast iron boilers are more resistant to corrosion than steel units. Water is the corrosive culprit, but its effect can be lessened with chemi-

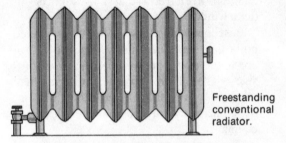

Freestanding conventional radiator.

cals. Proper water treatment can greatly prolong the life of steel boiler tubes. Consult an expert on this; water composition varies greatly in different parts of the country.

When you buy a boiler, make sure that it is "certified." Certified cast iron boilers are stamped "IBR" (Institute of Boiler and Radiator Manufacturers); steel boilers should be stamped "SBI" (Steel Boiler Institute). Most boilers are rated for both hot water and steam—check the nameplate. It's best to seek the advice of a reputable contractor when selecting a boiler.

Conventional radiators are set on the floor or mounted on the wall. More modern types are recessed in the wall. Recessed radiators should be backed with 1-inch insulation board, a sheet of reflective insulation, or both.

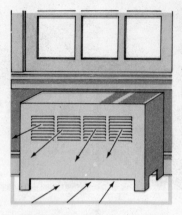 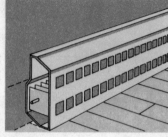 

Radiator cabinet (left), baseboard radiator (above), cabinet convector (right).

Radiators may be partially or fully enclosed by a cabinet. A full cabinet must have openings at top and bottom for air circulation. Preferred radiator location is under a window.

Baseboard radiators are hollow or finned units that resemble and take the place of conventional wood baseboards along outside walls. They provide uniform heat throughout a well-insulated room, with little temperature variation between floor and ceiling.

Convectors usually consist of finned tubes enclosed in a cabinet or baseboard unit with openings at top and bottom. Hot water or steam is circulated through the tubes. Air enters at the bottom of the enclosure, is heated by the tubes, and exits at the top. Some larger units include fans for forced air circulation. With this type of convector, summer cooling can be provided by adding a chiller and the necessary controls. Convectors are installed against an outside wall or recessed in a wall.

In a gravity hot-water heating system, the boiler must be located in the basement or crawl space, below the radiators. The supply line from the boiler to the radiators must have sufficient pitch or rise to induce circulation of the heated water. After the water gives off its heat in the radiators or convectors, it returns to the boiler through a separate return pipe line.

Because water expands when heated, an expansion tank must be provided in the system. In an "open" system, the tank is located above the highest radiator or convector and has an overflow pipe extending through the roof, thus exposing the water to the air. In a "closed" system, the expansion tank may be placed anywhere, but usually near the boiler. Half the tank is filled with air, which compresses when the heated water expands. Since the water is under pressure, the boiling point is raised. Higher temperatures can therefore be maintained without steam forming in the radiators, and smaller radiators can be used. There is little difference in fuel requirements between an open and a closed system.

Gravity systems require large supply and return mains; consequently, response to temperature changes is relatively slow because of the large volume of water in the pipes. Forced hot-water systems are considerably more efficient. A small booster or circulating pump forces the hot water through the pipes to the room radiators or convectors.

A one-pipe forced hot-water system utilizes a single pipe or main for both supply and return. It makes a complete circuit from the boiler through the system and back to the boiler. Two risers extend from the main to each room radiator or convector. In a two-pipe system, there are two

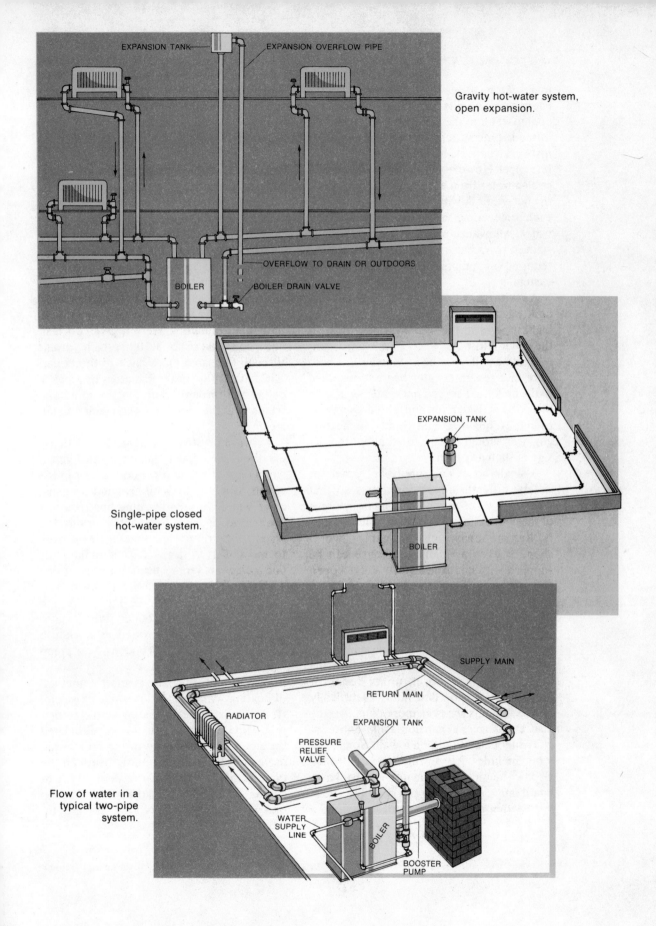

Gravity hot-water system, open expansion.

EXPANSION TANK

EXPANSION OVERFLOW PIPE

OVERFLOW TO DRAIN OR OUTDOORS

BOILER DRAIN VALVE

BOILER

Single-pipe closed hot-water system.

EXPANSION TANK

BOILER

Flow of water in a typical two-pipe system.

SUPPLY MAIN

RETURN MAIN

RADIATOR

EXPANSION TANK

PRESSURE RELIEF VALVE

WATER SUPPLY LINE

BOILER

BOOSTER PUMP

mains. One carries the heated water to the room-heating units; the other returns the cooled water to the boiler.

A one-pipe system is more economical to install since, as its name implies, it requires less pipe. However, in a one-pipe system, cooled water from each radiator mixes with the hot water flowing through the main, and each succeeding radiator receives cooler water. Allowance must be made for this in sizing the radiators—larger ones may be required at points farther along in the system.

As with gravity systems, an expansion tank must be provided, either above the highest point in the system (open) or near the boiler (closed).

Heating coils may be installed in the boiler or in a separate water heater connected to the boiler of a forced hot-water system to provide hot water for household use year-round. A qualified and reputable heating engineer should be consulted about the design of such a system.

A single boiler can supply hot water for several different circulation zones so that temperatures of individual rooms or areas of the house can be controlled independently. Remote areas such as a garage, workshop, or even a small greenhouse can be supplied with controlled heat. Valves open and close to direct the hot water in response to thermostat demands in the various zones of the house.

Gas- and oil-fired boilers for forced hot-water systems are compact and can be installed in an out-of-the-way corner of the basement or in a closet, utility room, or other space on the first floor. Electrically heated systems are even more compact; the heat exchanger, expansion tank, and controls may be mounted on a wall. Some systems include thermostatically controlled electric heating components in the baseboard units, eliminating the need for a central heating unit. Such a system may be a single loop installation circulating water by means of a pump, or it may be composed of individual sealed units filled with antifreeze solution. The sealed units depend on gravity flow of the solution in the unit. Each unit may have a thermostat, or several units may be controlled from one thermostat.

Steam heating systems are similar in concept and design to hot-water systems, but they are generally less popular for residential installations because they are less responsive to rapid changes in heat demands. In a one-pipe steam system, steam is generated in the boiler and delivered through a large main to pipes connecting to individual radiators. Here it gives off heat and condenses to water which drains through the same pipes back to the boiler. Air that may be in the radiators or pipes is exhausted through vents on the radiators, which emit the air but close on contact with steam.

A two-pipe steam heating system delivers the steam from the boiler through a supply line to radiators or convectors in the rooms, where it gives off heat and condenses to water. A separate pipe line from the lower end of each heat outlet drains the water to the return line that carries it back to the boiler. A trap at each radiator or convector prevents steam from returning with the water. Usually piping is arranged so that gravity provides the impetus for the water to return to the boiler. Where sufficient drop cannot be provided, as in a house without a basement, a condensation pump is installed for this purpose.

Radiant-panel heating is another method of heating with forced hot water or steam. (It is also a method of heating with electricity.) Hot water or steam is circulated through pipes concealed in the floor, wall, or ceiling. Heat is transmitted through the pipes to the surface of the floor, wall, or ceiling and from there to the room by radiation and convection. No outlets are re-

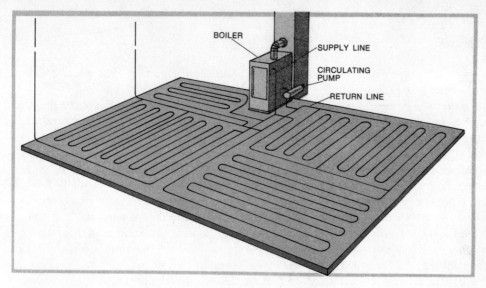

Radiant-panel heating.

quired — the floor, walls, or ceiling, in effect, act as radiators.

With radiant-panel heating, rooms are usually more comfortable at lower air temperatures than with other heating systems at higher air temperatures because temperatures are generally uniform throughout the room. This uniformity reduces body heat loss of the room's occupants and increases body comfort.

Underfloor radiant-panel heating systems are difficult to design, and the job should be left to a qualified engineer. A carpeted or bare wood floor, for example, might be very comfortable whereas a vinyl-covered kitchen floor or ceramic-tiled bathroom floor in the same system might be too hot, especially for bare feet. Panel heating in exterior walls requires adequate insulation behind to minimize heat loss. Ceiling panels, too, must be properly insulated unless you want to heat the space above the ceiling, as in a two-story house.

ELECTRIC HEATING

Electricity for house heating was first adopted in low-cost power areas such as the Tennessee Valley and the Pacific Northwest. A decade or so ago, improved equipment and techniques made electricity very competitive with flame fuels for heating in other parts of the country as well, and "all-electric" homes were highly touted. Convenience, cleanliness, even heat, safety, low maintenance cost, lack of noise or fumes, space saving, individual room temperature control, and many other advantages made it seem that electric heating was an idea whose time had come.

Then the "energy crunch" suddenly appeared. Utility companies, especially in the Northeast, that had been encouraging electric heat installations with lower rates for greater electrical usage, suddenly reversed these policies and penalized the electric heat users with higher rates. Owners of modestly sized all-electric homes in such areas as New England and New York found $300 and $400 monthly bills in their mailboxes. And that was several years before the record-breaking cold spells 1977–1978. Needless to say, electric heating systems rapidly declined in popularity.

Today, the cost of electricity in many areas proscribes the installation of new electric heating systems. Many utilities refuse to service such installations. (The same is true of gas-fired systems in some regions.) Still, hope must spring, and we hope and trust that solutions will be found to the energy problem, making it possible to more widely enjoy the many benefits of electric home heating systems.

There are many types and designs of electric house heating equipment. Electric baseboard units are designed for installation along the outside walls of each room in place of the baseboard at these locations. They come equipped with several different types of heating elements; some have supplementary sections with thermostats and convenience outlets. Provisions are made for wiring the heaters from the back, bottom, and ends and for connecting two or more sections. As many units as necessary may be assembled and installed, but the safe limits of the electric circuit must be considered. A 20-ampere house circuit with a 120-volt service can handle 2,400 watts. Most heaters consume between 1,000 and 2,500 watts (check the nameplate for this information). Make sure that your home's electrical system is adequate for this load (220-240 volt service is normally required).

Electric heating cable can be installed in new plastered ceilings or in new plaster over existing ceilings. The cable is laid back and forth, with spacing dependent on the heat-loss factor in the room to be heated.

Gypsum board panels with electric cable embedded are also available.

Central electric furnaces operate the same as conventional oil- or gas-fired systems. A typical unit consists of electric resistance heating elements, a fan, and thermostatic controls. Air is warmed as it passes over the heating coils and is usually forced by a fan into the rooms through a duct system. Depending on the need for heat, thermostats control the number of heating elements operating at one time. On a mild day, only one or two of the elements may be in use. During very cold weather, all the heating elements may come on to maintain the house temperature.

Electric heating units may be installed in the floor of a room and covered with a grille. These are usually used in front of hard-to-heat areas such as under floor-length picture windows and glass doors where it is impossible to install baseboard heaters. Heating is by convection from resistance heating elements.

Radiant and convection heating panels, equipped with various types of heating elements, are available for recessed or surface wall mounting. In the convection-type heater, warmed air is circulated either by gravity or by an electric fan. One or more of these wall units are installed in each room according to the heat requirements. Some have self-contained thermostats; others are controlled by wall thermostats. A grille should cover the front of the unit to prevent contact with the heating element.

Electric baseboard unit; partly cutaway view showing fins and wiring (left).

Heating cable in ceiling panels (below left).

Electric wall panels (below).

HEAT PUMPS

The heat pump is a single unit that both heats and cools. It works on the same principle as does a refrigerator. In a refrigerator, heat is taken out of the stored food and cabinet and expelled into the surrounding air. The heat pump extracts heat from the

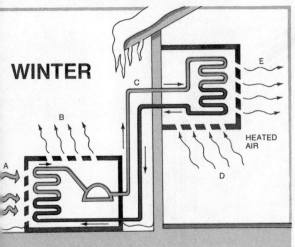
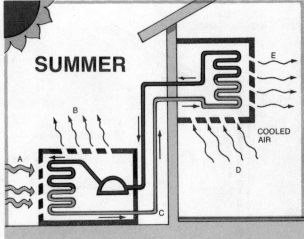

Heat-pump system.

A. Outside cold air.
B. Colder air expelled.
C. Heat extracted from outdoor air pumped inside.
D. Room air drawn in.
E. Warm air into room.

A. Outside warm air.
B. Warmer air expelled.
C. Cooled refrigerant pumped inside.
D. Room air drawn in.
E. Cold air into room.

outside air to warm a room or the entire house. A variation obtains heat from water in a well or pumped through a coil of pipes buried in the earth. As the heat is removed, the air or water is returned outside. Supplementary resistance heaters are usually used in conjunction with heat pumps to help heat the house during extremely cold weather.

In summer, the operation is reversed. Heat is removed from the air inside the house and discharged to the outside.

Heat pumps came on the market in a big way in the 1950's, and for a while it appeared that they were going to revolutionize home heating/cooling. Although the initial cost of a heat pump is higher than most other types of heating systems, it is efficient and clean and—except in colder climates— generally less expensive to operate. But problems plagued the devices. The units were noisy and vibrated excessively. Breakdowns were common and repairs expensive. The state of the art was not sufficiently advanced to make pumps that

could stand the wide range of temperatures encountered in year-round use. As a result, heat pumps virtually disappeared from the national market, maintaining sales only in the deep South.

A few years ago, a new generation of heat pumps appeared. The bugs had been eliminated, and the manufacturers were much more cautious in their marketing. Slowly the pumps have been making their way north, their progress helped by skyrocketing fuel costs and acute gas and oil shortages. Comparative figures invite dispute, but it would seem that in the long run the heat pump may well be more economical than other systems even in a cold climate. In any event, it is enjoying increasing popularity.

SOLAR HEATING

Somewhere on the horizon, as dazzling as a desert sunset, is the prospect of solar

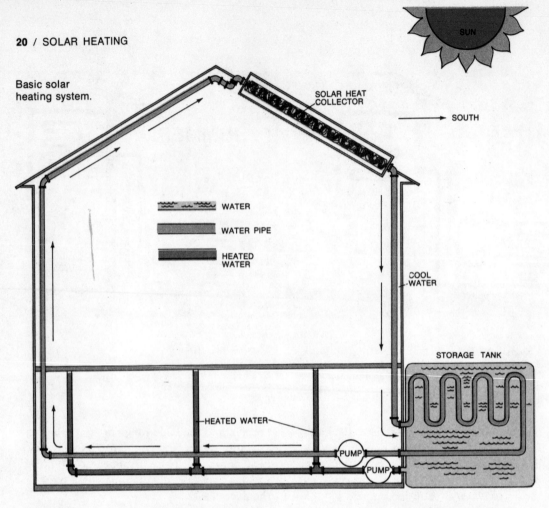

Basic solar
heating system.

SUN

SOLAR HEAT
COLLECTOR

→ SOUTH

WATER

WATER PIPE

HEATED
WATER

COOL
WATER

STORAGE TANK

HEATED WATER

PUMP

PUMP

heating. Scientists tell us that the amount of solar radiation striking the roof of a typical house in a single year is ten times greater than the house's annual heating demands. How to harness this radiation to provide heating and cooling inside the house had intrigued men for centuries. Although the technology in the field is still somewhat limited, the sense of urgency inspired by the energy crisis has led to some intense experimentation and innovative installations. Builders in various parts of the country have begun to offer solar-heated houses. But the systems currently available are, for the most part, prohibitively expensive for the average homeowner.

The parts of a solar heating system are relatively simple. A large, usually flat, panel is placed on the roof of the house, in a wall, or on the ground next to the house. The collector should be about half the size of the roof. It faces south and is tilted at approximately 45 degrees in the northern United States, flatter farther south.

As the sun's rays hit the collector, they heat either air or a water-antifreeze mixture that takes the heat into a storage tank. The tank, which is usually filled with water, must be fairly large—about 2,000-gallon capacity. The tank can also be filled with rocks to store the heat; in that case an even larger tank is required, and air, rather than water, brings the heat from the collector to the tank. The storage tank then serves as a source of heat for the distribution system, either a slightly modified forced-air or hot-water system or one specially designed for solar heating. In the summer, using an absorption system, the house can be cooled using the same heat.

There are many variations to the system. The walls and floors of the house itself may serve to store the heat, then warm the rooms by radiation. The Pueblo Indians used such a system to cope with the hot days and bitter cold nights in the Southwest. They built their dwellings with thick adobe walls that collected and stored the sun's heat, then radiated it to the inside to take away the chill of the night.

Another approach is to have solar cells in the roof, which react chemically when exposed to solar radiation, generating electricity which is then stored in batteries and used to power conventional heating (and cooling) systems. Although still in the early experimental stages, this type of application could be a breakthrough that might make solar heat economically feasible for residential use.

A solar heating system is rarely intended to fulfill all the heating needs of a house. The storage tank usually carries enough heat to get through a few overcast days and nights. After that, a conventional system must carry the heating load. Despite that, and despite its high initial cost, it is estimated that a solar heating system as available

today will pay for itself in a little more than ten years. As fuel costs continue to go up, that time will become shorter—the "fuel" costs of a solar heating system will never rise.

If solar heating for residences gains widespread favor, it will require some rethinking of local zoning ordinances. At present, few such laws would protect the owner of a solar-heated house from a neighbor's erecting a building or planting trees that would block the sun from his collectors, rendering his heating system useless. That would be the ultimate "spite fence," but neighbors have been known to do such things.

Many companies have jumped into the budding solar energy field, not all of them of unquestionable character. Since the technology is new and not widely known, it is inevitable that some fast-buck hustlers and outright crooks have come on the scene, making exaggerated promises of performance and economy in pushing "solar heat" on homeowners whose sales resistance has been greatly weakened by the shockingly high costs of conventional heating fuels. As ever, let the buyer beware. If you wish to explore the possibilities of using the sun to help heat your house, deal only with reputable and knowledgeable manufacturers and contractors—who, at this stage, are still few and far between.

2

Fuels

O VER THE CENTURIES, man has burned a number of fuels to keep himself warm, among them animal fat, wood, dried manure, peat, charcoal, bones, coke, coal, oil, and gas. The latter two are most widely used today, and it wasn't too long ago that you could depend on lively arguments between proponents of each fuel whenever the subject came up at a gathering of homeowners—which was "cleaner," which was more economical, which was all-around "better." Today these same homeowners are more likely to sympathize with each other about the astronomical fuel costs and the shrinking availability of both oil and gas in many areas. And the diehard who has clung to his coal furnace may laugh at both of them as he ponders his wisdom in the warmth of a home heated with a fuel that is in relative abundance.

Modern heating equipment is generally efficient when used with the fuel for which it was designed. But even with modern equipment, some fuels cost more than others to do the same job. Although cost comparisons vary widely according to geographical area and fuel availability, it is possible to set some general guidelines for determining which fuel will be most economical. Electricity, although not a fuel, must also be considered because of its increasing popularity for heating homes.

COMPARING FUEL COSTS

A few terms must be understood to make the comparisons. As a basic unit of measurement, a Btu (British thermal unit) is defined as the quantity of heat required to raise the temperature of one gram of water one degree Fahrenheit. (As this country is approaching the metric age, we should inform you that a calorie is the quantity of heat required to raise the temperature of one gram of water one degree Centigrade; one Btu is the equivalent of 252 calories.) A therm is 100,000 Btu's.

The therms of heat per dollar should not be the sole consideration in selecting a heating fuel. Installation cost, the efficiency with which each unit converts fuel into useful heat, and the insulation level of the house should also be considered. For example, electrically heated houses usually have twice the insulation thickness (a one-time expense), particularly in the ceiling and floor, and therefore may require considerably less heat input than houses heated with fuel-burning systems. To compare costs properly, efficiency of combustion and heat value of the fuel must be known.

Heating units vary in efficiency depending upon type, method of operation, condition, and location. Gas- and oil-fired steam and hot-water boilers of current design, operated under favorable conditions, have 70 to 80 percent efficiency. Forced warm-air furnaces with gas burners or atomizing oil burners generally provide about 80 percent efficiency in converting the fuel to heat. Oil-fired furnaces with the less expensive pot-type burners usually develop not over 70 percent efficiency. Stoker-fired coal furnaces range from 60 to 75 percent efficiency. Electricity is rated at 100 percent efficiency because there is no chimney and usually no ductwork through which heat may be lost. Proponents of other fuels point out that this is "in-house" efficiency and does not take into account the use of other fuel at the electrical powerhouse that went into generating the electricity. But for our purposes, the in-house figure is valid, although conservationists may think otherwise.

You can figure the comparative costs of various fuels and electricity based on local prices by using the table on this page. The efficiency of electricity, oil, gas, and coal is taken as 100, 75, 75, and 65 percent respectively. The efficiencies may actually be higher (except for electricity) or lower, depending upon conditions, but these values are reasonable.

The heat values in the table are taken as

3,413 Btu per kilowatt hour (kwh) of electricity for resistance heating; 139,000 Btu per gallon of No. 2 fuel oil (the grade most commonly used for home heating); 1,050 Btu per cubic foot of natural gas; 92,000 Btu per gallon of propane (LP) gas; and 13,000 Btu per pound of coal.

More Btu's of heat per kilowatt hour can generally be obtained with a heat pump installation than with resistance heating units. The difference varies depending on outside temperature and other factors. In warm climates, heat pumps may need only about half as much electricity as resistance heaters. In the very cold climates of the northerly states, the heat pump may use as much electric energy as is required for resistance heating.

For the person in the market for a new heating system, fuel cost comparisons are at best a vague, albeit important, guideline. As anyone who has had to pay fuel bills during the past three or four winters is painfully aware, prices can fluctuate (invariably upward) wildly over the course of a heating season. Relative costs provide a good take-off point, but perhaps a more vital consideration is the likelihood of continued availability of the fuel. At the present time, new electric and gas heating installations are barred by some utility companies. This situation is likely to ease, but what the future holds is uncertain. Check out the conditions and prospects in your region before making any decision on heating fuel.

Fuel	Quantity to supply one therm of heat	Multiply values in column 2 by local costs per	Comparative costs per therm of heat
Electricity	29.3 kwh	kwh	——————
Fuel oil	.96 gal.	gal.	——————
Natural gas	127 cu. ft.	cu. ft.	——————
LP gas (propane)	1.45 gal.	gal.	——————
Coal	11.8 lbs. (.006 ton)	ton	——————

OIL

Oil in one form or another has been used as a heating fuel for a very long time. Around the turn of the century, the technology had advanced as far as the kerosene heaters that were providing cold-weather comfort for households throughout the United States. Then, in the early 1920's, the first automatic oil burner heralded a new era of comfort control, allowing the home's occupants to select the desired temperature by the mere touch of a thermostat. Those early automatic burners were remarkably sophisticated, and the basic design, with modifications, is still in widespread use today.

Oil requires no handling and little space for storing—often the storage tank is buried in the ground. It leaves no ash and burns "clean"—the combustion chamber is sealed off from the heat exchanger so that combustion by-products cannot enter the distribution system.

Two grades of fuel oil are used for home heating. No. 1 is lighter and somewhat more expensive than the far more common No. 2, which has higher heat value per gallon. The nameplate or instruction booklet that comes with the oil burner indicates what grade of fuel is to be used. In general, No. 1 is used in pot-type burners and No. 2 in gun- and rotary-type burners.

There are two kinds of oil burners: vaporizing and atomizing. Vaporizing burners premix the oil vapor with air. The pot-type vaporizing burner consists of a pot containing a pool of oil. An automatic or handset valve regulates the amount of oil in the pot. Heat from the flame vaporizes the oil. In some heaters, a pilot flame or electric arc ignites the oil pot when heat is required; in earlier models, the oil is ignited manually and burns at any set fuel rate between high and low fire until shut off. There are few moving parts, and operation is quiet. Some pot-type burners do not even require electric power.

Atomizing burners are of two general types: gun (pressure) and rotary. The gun burner is by far the more popular for residential heating applications. It has a pump that forces oil through an atomizing nozzle. A fan blows air into the oil fog, and an electric spark ignites the mixture, which burns in a refractory-lined firepot. This is the type of oil burner used in most modern residential oil heating installations.

The future of oil as a heating fuel is wrapped up in national, international, and industrial politics. Boycotts, embargos, depletion allowances, offshore and onshore drilling rights, supertanker economics—these and other murky matters will determine the availability, as well as the affordability, of heating oil in the years ahead.

GAS

Three kinds of gas—natural, manufactured, and bottled—are used for residential heating. Bottled gas (usually propane) is referred to as LPG (liquefied petroleum gas) or simply LP. It has been gaining in popularity as a heating fuel, especially in rural areas where other fuels are less readily available. Different gases have different heat values when burned. A burner adjusted for one type of gas must be readjusted when another gas is used.

The room thermostat controls a valve that feeds the gas to the burner. A pilot light is needed for combustion. The pilot may be lighted at the beginning of the heating season and shut off when the crocuses and rosebuds appear. It may also be kept burning year-round, helping to prevent condensation during nonheating seasons that will hasten corrosion of metal parts of the furnace. However, this latter practice is now being discouraged by energy conservationists, who claim that the cumulative waste of

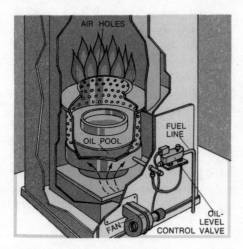

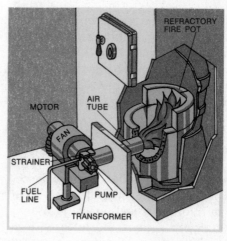

Pot-type vaporizing oil burner (far left).

Gun-type atomizing oil burner (left).

gas resources by year-round pilot burning is horrendous.

The pilot light should be equipped with a safety thermostat to prevent the gas valve from opening if the pilot goes out; no gas can then escape into the house. (Pilot lights of all gas-burning appliances—water heaters, clothes dryers, ranges—should be equipped with similar safety devices.)

Conversion gas burners may be used in boilers and furnaces designed for other fuels if they have adequate heating surfaces and are properly gas-tight. All gas burners should be installed by competent, experienced heating contractors, closely following manufacturer's directions. Gas-burning equipment should bear the seal of the American Gas Association.

Gas-burning furnaces must be vented to the outside. Keep chimneys and smokepipes free from leaks. Connect electrical controls for gas-burning equipment to a separate switch so that the circuit can be quickly shut down in case of trouble. Gas burners should be cleaned, inspected, and properly adjusted annually. Gas is a clean, trouble-free, and safe fuel, but it does have dangerous and explosive potential if used incorrectly or carelessly. Even the most painstaking safeguards can be compromised by foolishness. Don't be foolish.

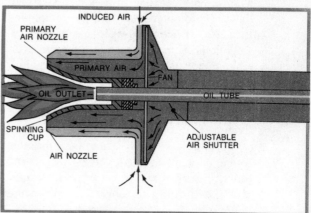

Rotary-type atomizing oil burner.

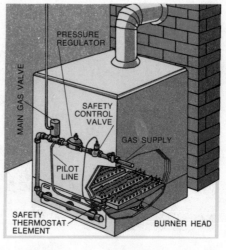

Gas burner, room thermostat controlled.

Bottled gas is heavier than air. If it leaks into the basement, it will accumulate at the lowest point and create a hazard. When using bottled gas, make sure that the safety control valve is so placed that it shuts off the gas to the pilot light as well as the burner when the pilot goes out.

ELECTRICITY

Electric heating offers convenience, cleanliness, evenness of heat, safety, and freedom from odors and fumes. It also offers, in many regions, ridiculously high electric bills because of a power shortage that has prompted many utility companies to refuse service to new electric heating installations. Some of these utilities are even encouraging users of electric heat to switch to competitive fuels—the same homeowners that they were wooing a few years back with promises of low-cost "all-electric" living.

Nevertheless, electric heating continues to be popular in those areas where the power crunch is not so acute, and presumably it will return to other areas when the energy situation gets sorted out, as it must.

Houses that are heated electrically must be well insulated and weatherstripped. Windows should be double- or triple-glazed, and walls, floors, and ceilings should be vapor-sealed. The required insulation, weatherproofing, and vapor barriers can easily be provided in new homes but may be difficult to add to older houses. No chimney is needed for electric heat.

The heating equipment should be only large enough to handle the heat load. Oversized equipment costs more both initially and in operation and requires heavier wiring than does properly sized equipment.

COAL

Coal has a somewhat spotty history as a heating fuel. Its combustible qualities were known to the early Greeks, yet through the centuries it was seldom used. In coal-rich England, burning coal was made a capital offense in the 14th century, and at least one man was executed for transgressing the law. Queen Elizabeth I changed all. that, and London effectively became one big smudgepot—but its residents (at least those who could afford shelter and coal) were snug and warm, if somewhat sooty.

From early in this century until the

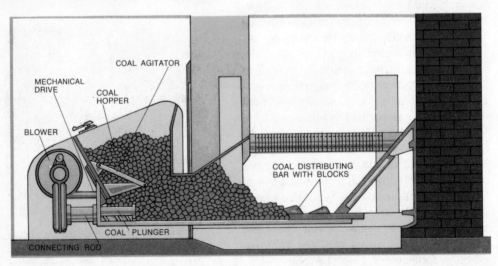

Coal stoker fire burner.

MECHANICAL DRIVE

COAL AGITATOR

COAL HOPPER

BLOWER

COAL DISTRIBUTING BAR WITH BLOCKS

COAL PLUNGER

CONNECTING ROD

1940's, coal was the staple fuel throughout much of the United States, and the coal bin was a space-consuming fixture in many basements. Homeowners whose driveways were not adequate to bear the weight of the delivery truck would have the coal (usually in quantities of one or two tons) dumped in the street, from where it became a family project to move it by shovel and wheelbarrow to the "coal window" outside the basement bin. Several generations of Americans developed their muscles in this way. Who needed health spas?

Gas and oil shoved coal far into the background as a residential heating fuel during the post-World War II building boom. But the sudden and critical fuel shortage of a few years ago catapulted coal into prominence again, at least as an alternative to be considered. Although few people actually converted from gas, oil, or electricity to coal as a heating fuel, those who still heated with coal furnaces had their day and most have decided to stick with coal "for the duration" until they see what the future fuel situation will be. Since the nation's coal reserves are quite extensive, it is just possible that coal may be the fuel of the future, at least the immediate future, as well as that of the past.

Two kinds of coal are used for home heating: anthracite (hard) and bituminous (soft). Anthracite coal sizes are standardized, bituminous are not. Heat value of different sizes of coal varies little, but certain sizes are better suited for burning in firepots of given sizes and depths. If you burn coal, your supplier can advise you on this.

Both anthracite and bituminous coal are used in stoker firing (stokers automatically feed the coal to the furnace, relieving the homeowner of the tedious shovel-wielding that plagued his grandfather morning and night). Stokers may be installed at the front, side, or rear of a furnace or boiler. Space must be allowed for servicing the stoker and for cleaning the furnace. Furnaces and boilers with horizontal heating surfaces require frequent cleaning, because fly ash (a fine, powdery substance) collects on these surfaces. Follow manufacturer's directions for operating stokers.

Although coal furnaces of recent manufacture are considerably improved over earlier models, they still create dirt and grime, which can be transmitted throughout the house. Still, they must be considered as an alternative if crunch comes to crash in the energy situation.

WOOD

Wood, probably man's first heating fuel, deserves at least passing mention, although its use today is usually limited to rustic cabin stoves and home fireplaces, which are intended primarily for aesthetics and only secondarily as supplemental sources of warmth. The use of wood requires more labor and more storage space than do other fuels. And, unless you can chop your own, wood costs are, like other fuels, almost out of sight, especially in such unforested areas as New York City, Chicago, Los Angeles, and other major urban centers. On the plus side, wood fires are easy to start, burn with little smoke, and leave little ash.

Most well-seasoned hardwoods have about half the heat value per pound as that of good coal. A cord (equivalent to a stack of cut firewood 4 by 4 by 8 feet, or 128 cubic feet) of hickory, oak, beech, sugar maple, or rock elm weighs roughly two tons and has about the same heat value as a ton of good coal.

FUTURE FUELS

Although it is unlikely that new heating fuels will be discovered in the immediate future, the pressures created by the rapid depletion of natural resources and by international politics will spur developments along this line. Much research has already been done in solar heating (see CHAPTER 1). Many other areas have been explored as well. Some may bear fruit.

One potentially fruitful experiment literally grew on trees. The town of Brookhaven, New York, collected hundreds of thousands of cubic yards of leaves for its Composting Center. As any good greenthumber knows, the center of a compost pile generates a lot of heat as the organic material decomposes. Brookhaven decided to utilize this heat by running a copper pipe through the pile and into a large greenhouse on the site. The results have been "gratifying," although town officials don't recommend that you throw away your present heating unit and depend on the leaves of autumn to offset the cold of winter—at least not yet.

Although a lot of the ideas that have been put forward for sources of heat fall into the crackpot category, many of them warrant further study. Tapping the wind as a producer of energy—and, consequently, heat—is certainly not new, but it is coming under fresh scrutiny by universities, utilities, industry, private individuals, and the federal government. Several experimental facilities have already been built, and results are being carefully studied. In the New Mexico desert, a 170-foot-high vertical axis wind turbine, resembling an upside-down eggbeater, is being tested by the Federal Energy Research and Development Administration. If it checks out, the device will generate electric power that can be utilized for residential heating.

Not only the wind above but the heat below are prospects for heating your home. Several miles beneath the earth's surface are magmas, or steam chambers, which scientists are looking at with renewed interest as heat sources. In Reykjavík, Iceland, where the chambers are relatively close to the surface, most of the city's heating needs are supplied by these subterranean sources.

Some farther-out suggestions for future fuel sources seem somewhat further away as well. These include the conversion of old tires into fuel oil and the recovery of gas from garbage and (back to the basics) manure. Although all these schemes are technologically feasible, their implementation seems economically prohibitive at present. Tomorrow? Who can say?

For now, the most promising possibility seems to be the sun. With the heavy emphasis being given to solar heat research projects, advances will almost surely be made that will bring the cost of installing this type of residential heating within the reach of the average homeowner—and then the choice will be much more attractive.

Beyond that? Nuclear fuel is almost certainly in the offing, although nobody can say at this time exactly when. There are well over 200 nuclear generating plants already in operation or under construction in this country, but the true capabilities and limitations of nuclear power are yet to be fully evaluated. Most likely, the benefits of nuclear power will be utilized in terms of more readily available power for the home heating system; but a more direct method of nuclear heating may yet be devised.

Such exotic thoughts of future fuels won't keep you and your family warm next winter. If you are in the market for a new heating system, your fuel choices are still among gas, oil, electricity, and possibly coal, with a consideration given to that friendly old sun as a supplementary source of warmth.

3

Heating System Controls

OUR PRIMITIVE forebears may have discovered fire as a source of heat, but controlling it was something else. They knew that rubbing two sticks together turned on the heat, and they soon learned that water carried from the nearby stream in a brontosaurus-skin bucket would douse it. But the idea that someone might simply turn a dial pointer to 60 or 65 or 70 or whatever and then sit back while the heating system delivered that exact degree of heat would have been totally incomprehensible to them—as it was to most people until quite recently. Remember this the next time you adjust your heating system's thermostat.

THERMOSTATS

In its simplest form, a thermostat is a bimetallic switch, made of two pieces of dissimilar metals that expand at different temperatures. One piece is usually brass, which expands quickly when heated, and the other may be invar (an alloy of nickel and steel), which heats and expands much more slowly. The two fused metal pieces remain in place when cool, completing an electrical circuit. Under heat conditions, tension between the two metals expanding at different temperatures causes the fused strip to bend. When it reaches a temperature level indicated by the thermostat's selector dial, one end of the bimetallic strip rises far enough to lose contact with the circuit. The power is thus severed, and the furnace burner or electric heat current is shut off. As it cools, the metal regains its

original shape until it again closes the circuit, and heating resumes.

Since the thermostat (or thermostats, in the case of a zoned system) controls the

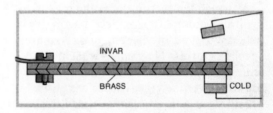

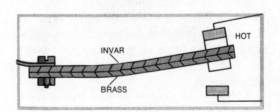

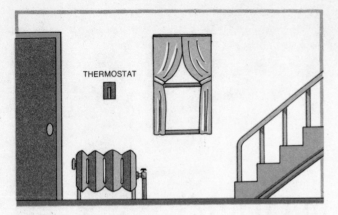

Bad thermostat location.

house temperature, common sense dictates that it must be properly located. This usually means on an inside wall and away from cold walls or doors that open to the outside. Other locations to avoid are the foot of an open stairway (too much draft), above a heat register, lamp, or television set (excessive heat will negate its function), or where it will be affected by direct heat from the sun. If you suspect a thermostat's accuracy, it's a good idea to check it against a good thermometer.

LIMIT CONTROLS

Although the thermostat is the most recognizable control in a modern heating system, each type of heating plant requires special controls. No matter what the system, there should be a high-limit control to prevent overheating. These are usually provided, or at least recommended, by the manufacturer.

The high-limit control, which is usually another thermostat, shuts down the system before a furnace, boiler, or other type of heating unit becomes dangerously or wastefully hot. In steam systems, it responds to pressure; in other systems, it responds to temperature.

A high-limit control is often combined with fan or pump controls in forced-air or forced hot-water systems. These may be set to start the fan or the pump circulating when the furnace or boiler warms up and to stop it when the heating plant cools down. They are ordinarily set just high enough to reach, without surpassing, the desired temperature and can be adjusted to suit weather conditions.

Forced-air systems can be set for continuous air circulation (CAC). The fan or blower will run continuously at a slow speed, while the burner responds to temperature changes inside the house. This minimizes temperature fluctuations and provides a more even warmth for maximum year-round comfort.

OIL BURNER CONTROLS

The controls for an oil burner allow electricity to pass through the motor and ignition transformer and shut them off in the proper order. They also stop the motor if the oil does not ignite or if the flame goes out for any reason. This is accomplished by means of another thermostat built into the relay. The sensing element of the stack control is inserted into the smokepipe near the furnace or boiler. Some heating units are equipped with electric eye (cadmium sulfide) flame detectors, which are used in place of the stack control.

Without the protection of the stack thermostat or electric eye, a gun- or rotary-type burner could flood the basement with oil if

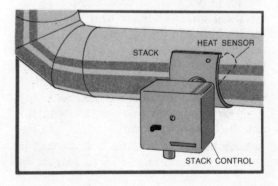

it failed to ignite—and the occasional horror stories that one reads in the newspapers about oil being mistakenly delivered to the wrong address testify to the fact that this is a slimy mess to be avoided at whatever cost. With the stack or eye control, the relay allows the motor to run only a short time if the oil fails to ignite; then it opens the motor circuit and keeps it open until it is manually reset. If the trouble persists, it will again shut down the system. By then, you should get the clue.

STOKER-FIRED COAL BURNER CONTROLS

The control system for a coal stoker is much like that for an oil burner. However, an automatic timer is usually included to operate the stoker for a few minutes every half hour or so to keep the fire alive during cool (not cold) weather when little heat is required.

A stack thermostat need not be used, but it is advisable in the event that a power failure might allow an untended fire to go out. Otherwise, the stoker will fill the cold firepot with coal when the power comes on again. An electric eye can also monitor this. In a stoker-control setup for a forced-air system, the furnace thermostat can act as high-limit and fan control.

OTHER HEATING SYSTEM CONTROLS

In some forced hot-water systems, especially those that also provide domestic hot water, a mixing valve is used. The water temperature of the boiler is maintained at some high fixed value, such as 200 degrees Fahrenheit. Only a portion of this high-temperature water is circulated through the heating system. Some of the water flowing through the radiators or convectors by-

passes the boiler. The amount of hot water admitted is controlled by a differential thermostat operating in the range between outdoor and indoor temperatures. This installation is more expensive than the more commonly used control systems, but it responds almost immediately to demands made upon it. Although it cannot anticipate temperature changes (even the computers do poorly at that), it is to a measure regulated by outside temperatures, which change earlier than those indoors.

The flow of hot air or hot water to various parts of the house can be separately controlled. This zoning—maintaining rooms or sections of the house at different desired temperatures—can be used for such purposes as maintaining sleeping quarters at lower temperatures than living areas. Fuel savings help to offset the initial higher cost of these more elaborate control systems. Once again, the advice of a competent and reputable professional is strongly recommended when mapping out a zoning system for your house.

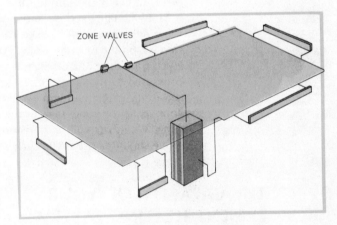

ZONE VALVES

Two-zone hot-water system.

Controls for **gas burners** and **electric heating units** are integral parts of the units themselves. They have been detailed in the preceding chapters: HEATING SYSTEMS, and FUELS.

4

Heating a New or Remodeled Space

SOONER OR LATER, most families seem to outgrow the confines of the old homestead. Children graduate from the playpen, so a playroom is needed if the rest of the house is to be spared the noise and havoc that accompany preteen and adolescent years. More bedrooms are also needed to accommodate the burgeoning family. Perhaps the family life-style and fortunes have changed, and the need is simply for more room. Not too long ago, the solution would probably be to "pick up and move up," but the skyrocketing cost of housing and high mortgage interest rates make this less attractive these days. Besides, there are other good reasons for staying put: friends, familiarity, and maybe just because it's a nice neighborhood. So more and more people are finding new space within their present homes, or adding on to them, rather than "movin' on."

Many housing styles — most notably the story-and-a-half "Cape Cod" and some split-level and "raised ranch" designs — make allowances for expansion within the existing walls. An attic may be finished, or an upper or lower level, providing one or several new rooms. Or a garage or basement may be converted to living space, assuming they are dry and weatherproof. More ambitious projects might include raising the roof to gain second- or third-floor space, or knocking out the walls to enlarge a room or add a whole new wing. Whatever your expansion plans may be, a method of heating the new space should figure in the early stages.

THE CAPACITY OF YOUR PRESENT HEATING SYSTEM

Perhaps the furnace that presently heats your home is adequate to heat the new space as well. Sometimes a contractor installs a furnace with additional capacity, especially in a house designed with expansion in mind. But this is definitely not always the case, and if you try to overburden a furnace that is already working at peak capacity, you are asking for trouble — and will surely get it. At best, the heat will be uneven, not only in the new space but throughout the system. Eventually, overworked burners will succumb to early demise.

A "heat loss calculation" should be made

of your home, including the planned expansion space, to determine whether the existing furnace is up to carrying an increased load. This involves some complicated formulas and, unless you are a graduate physicist or a mathematical marvel, is better left to the slide-rule savants. Most fuel oil companies and utilities can supply you with the information you need. Or you can contact a reputable heating contractor for advice on your present system's capacity.

If the new space is within the existing walls of the house or if only a small room extension is added, perhaps only a minor relocation of ductwork or piping and heat supply outlets will be needed. You can probably do this work yourself. If your house is uninsulated or underinsulated, you may be able to, in effect, increase the present system's capacity by adequately insulating both new and old areas (see CHAPTER 7). By helping the furnace do its job better and more efficiently, you will also be adding to its capabilities, perhaps enough to offset the additional burden of the new space.

EXTENDING A WARM-AIR SYSTEM

If you are sure that the existing furnace can "take the heat" of the additional load, it is not very difficult to extend the ductwork or pipes to new outlets. Tools you'll need are an "aircraft" snips, an old screwdriver or cold chisel, a ball peen or tinsmith's hammer, a drill, and a keyhole saw. A tin snips will also come in handy. Always be very careful when working with sheet metal—it can cut like a razor, and even worse because of jagged edges that are almost unavoidable when cutting. It is recommended that you exercise that ounce of caution by wearing a heavy, long-sleeved shirt and work gloves whenever you might come in contact with the sharp metal edges.

If you have a gravity warm-air heating system, you must locate a spot on the plenum—the "bonnet" on top of the furnace—where you can "tap in." For heat runs to the first and second floors, 8-inch or 9-inch pipes are usually used; 24-inch lengths in these sizes, with one end crimped so that it can be fitted into the other end of an adjoining section, are available at many hardware stores or at heating supply outlets (although you may have to shop around, since some of the latter sell only to contractors). Using

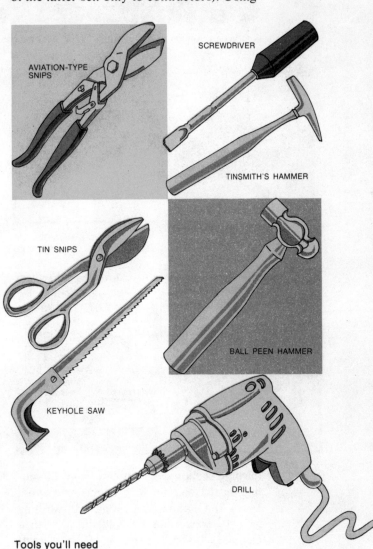

AVIATION-TYPE SNIPS

SCREWDRIVER

TINSMITH'S HAMMER

TIN SNIPS

BALL PEEN HAMMER

KEYHOLE SAW

DRILL

Tools you'll need

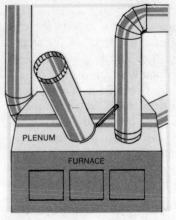

1. Draw an outline on the plenum.

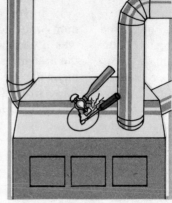

2. Make a gash in the metal.

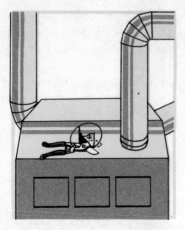

3. Cut out with aircraft snips.

4. Draw a pencil line around the pipe.

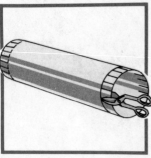

5. Make snips-cuts into the line.

6. Bend out every other tab to a 90-degree angle.

7. Fit the unbent tabs inside the hole.

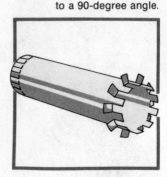

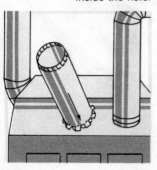

the pipe section as a template, draw an outline on the plenum with pencil or crayon. Inside the outline, make a gash by striking an old screwdriver or cold chisel with a hammer. Insert the point of an aircraft snips into the gash and cut out the hole following the marked line. (There are three basic configurations of aircraft snips, called "right-hand," "left-hand," and "center-cut." Right-hand cut in a counterclockwise direction and are generally favored for most usage. Left-hand cut in the clockwise direction and are used primarily when obstacles prevent the use of right-hand snips; southpaws often prefer to do most cutting with left-hand snips. Center-cuts are a compromise, and are perfectly suited for most do-it-yourself purposes — why buy three, if one will do? But they are not satisfactory for cutting holes of less than 6-inch diameter.)

A length of pipe — or in some cases, an elbow, depending on where the heat run is going — is then connected into this hole. Make a pencil mark all around the pipe or elbow approximately ¾ inch in from the uncrimped end. Use the aircraft snips or tin snips to make cuts approximately ¾ inch apart in to this line, all around the pipe. Bend out every other tab to a 90-degree angle, taking care not to cut yourself in the process. Fit the unbent tabs inside the hole in the plenum, then reach through the pipe and bend them over inside to lock the pipe in place. It's not really necessary, but you can further anchor it by drilling holes through a few of the outer tabs and the plenum and driving in sheet-metal screws.

A damper should be installed inside the pipe near the furnace, so that you can control the flow of hot air through the run, helping to balance the entire system. Dampers are available at heating supply outlets and many hardware stores, or you can make your own by cutting a circle of sheet metal to a diameter about $3/8$ inch less than that of the pipe. Various types of handles are available; attach one to the edge of the damper, then place the damper inside the pipe, with the handle inserted through a hole drilled in the pipe.

Additional pipes and elbows are then added to lead the run to its outlet, with the crimped end of one length fitting into the uncrimped end of the next. Elbows are usually made in four sections and are adjustable from 90 degrees to straight, so you should have no trouble getting the run where you want it to go. One or two sheet-metal screws at each joint will hold it all together. Pipe runs should be pitched upward (this is gravity heat, remember). Long runs can be supported by wire loops nailed to the joists at intervals of approximately 4 feet.

For first-floor installations, the pipe enters a fitting that is attached to a wall or floor register. For upper-floor rooms, the pipe must connect with a duct or riser that carries the heat through a first-floor partition to the higher levels. If you have a house that was designed for expansion, a thoughtful contractor may have installed such a riser—unconnected to the furnace— when the house was being built. It takes only a few minutes and costs just a few dollars at that stage, before the walls are enclosed, but it saves a lot of grief for you at this stage. If you are not so fortunate, you have a real job on your hands. But with patience, it can be done.

First, you must find a location for the ris-

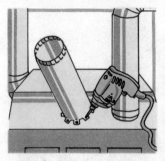
8. Secure with metal screws.

9. Cut sheet metal damper

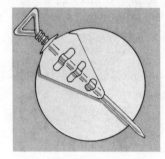
10. Attach handle.

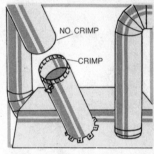
11. Fit pipes together.

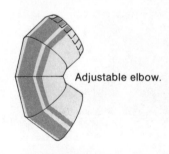
Adjustable elbow.

12. Pitch pipe runs upward; support them with wire loops.

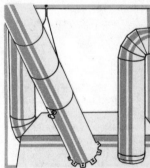

13. Connect pipe to first-floor registers (right).

14. Riser connection for upper floors (below).

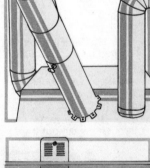

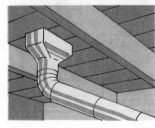

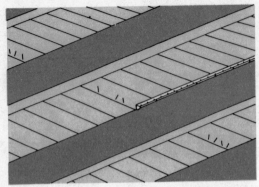

15. Measure carefully to find the partition. (Note nails penetrating the subfloor.)

16. Saw out subfloor and floor plate (above).

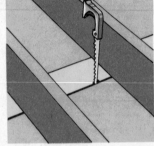

17. Cut out top plate from attic (above right).

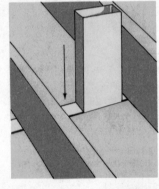

18. Slide in the riser through the cut-out (right).

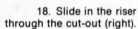

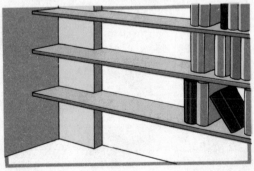

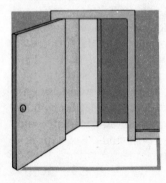

Riser cleverly concealed as part of a bookshelf (far left).

Riser run unobtrusively through a closet (left).

er. It must run between the studs of a partition, as close to the furnace as possible, and preferably to a point where it can be connected to a register in the upper-floor room. Otherwise, horizontal ducts will be needed beneath the second floor, cutting down the flow of heat. Wall registers are normally preferred, but it may be better to install a floor register than to have the heat turn so many corners. Stay away from stud channels that are crossed by electrical wiring or contain outlets or switches. You can check this by looking on the first floor, and by observing where wires disappear from the basement into the floor above.

Carefully measure on the first floor and in the basement to find the partition; you can usually corroborate your figurings by noting nails penetrating the subfloor where the partition plate is fastened. If you are unsure, remove the shoe molding along the partition and drill or drive nails through the subfloor, then note their locations in the basement. Drill pilot holes from below and saw out the subfloor and the plate to make room for the riser (usually $3\frac{1}{4} \times 10$ or $3\frac{1}{4} \times 12$ inches).

With a flashlight, carefully inspect the between-studs wall cavity to make sure that no wires run across it. If there are wires, shift the riser location—that is a lot easier than trying to move the wires. If the passageway is clear, proceed to the second floor to continue the operation.

Again, carefully measure and cut an

Chapter 4 ● Heating a New or Remodeled Space

opening in the top plate of the first-floor partition to match that cut in the basement. Now slide the riser down through the cutout (or up from the basement), hook up the basement piping, and use duct or pipe as necessary to lead from the riser to a wall or floor register.

You may be able to shortcut this somewhat tedious operation if there is a closet or utility room on the first floor through which you can unobtrusively run the riser without having to work inside the walls. Or if you run into insoluble problems trying to run the riser inside the walls—perhaps you simply can't find an open space uncluttered with wiring or pipes—you may prefer to run it outside the wall in a corner of a first-floor room and box around it, or conceal it as part of a built-in bookshelf or cabinet.

A gravity system is not very effective for heating a basement room. It operates on the principle of hot air going up, but you want the heat to go down in a basement room. At best, you may be able to heat the upper reaches of the room, but the floor will almost surely remain too cold for comfort.

Ductwork for a forced-air system is usually "stepped down" in width as each individual heat run or branch line (usually 4- to 6-inch pipe) is "taken off." To add to such a run without stepping down (which would require new ductwork), cut a hole in the side of the duct, using aircraft snips as described earlier. To divert air to your new takeoff, you can install a small baffle inside

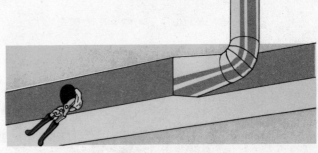

1. Cut a hole in the side of the duct.

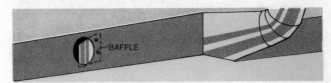

2 Install a small baffle inside the duct.

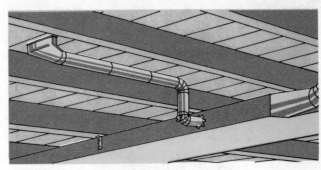

3. Lead the run to a first-floor outlet.

the duct. This is simply a bent piece of metal shaped to catch the air flow and is held in place by sheet-metal screws. With the baffle in place, attach a piece of pipe or an elbow to the hole in the duct by dovetailing the end as above. Install a damper, then lead the run to a first-floor outlet (usually on

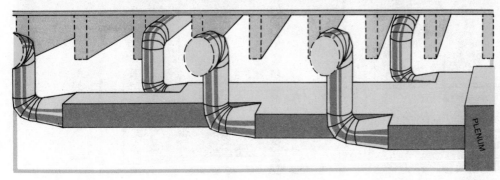

"Stepped-down" ductwork.

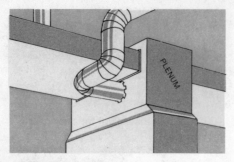

Cut into plenum to run pipe to a first- or second-floor heat outlet.

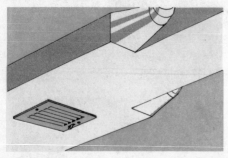

Basement outlet in duct.

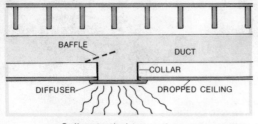

Collars to tie heat outlet to new ceiling.

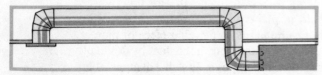

New heat run for basement room.

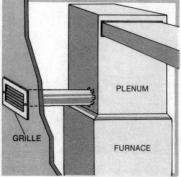

Heat run off plenum.

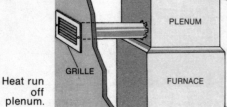

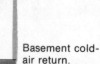

Basement cold-air return.

the outer wall) or to a riser leading to the second floor. The methods of installation are the same as for a gravity system.

You may also be able to cut into the plenum of a forced-air furnace to run pipe to a first- or second-floor heat outlet. As above, a baffle may be needed to divert the flow of air toward the new run. This is especially necessary when a main duct line runs off the same side of the plenum.

A forced-air system offers several possibilities for heating a basement room. If the ductwork passes through the area to be heated, you can install a register or registers by cutting into the bottom or side of the duct and fastening with sheet-metal screws. Some types of registers will divert the heated air when they are opened; others may require a baffle inside the duct. If the ductwork is to be boxed in as part of the basement finishing, you can have short collars made at a sheet-metal shop to bring the registers level with the surface of the new ceiling.

Where ductwork does not run through the new living space but is off to one side of the basement, a new heat run can be tapped into the side or (where accessible) the top of the duct. Pipe is then run between the joists to a ceiling register, or down through or behind a partition to a wall outlet. Again, a baffle may be needed inside the duct.

You may also tap directly into the plenum to heat the basement room, especially

Chapter 4 ● Heating a New or Remodeled Space

if it is adjacent to the furnace. You may be able to run a short collar from the plenum to a wall register in the room to provide comfortable heating.

Since a forced-air heating system depends on the circulation of air by means of a fan, it follows that, when you increase its output of heated air by adding new outlets, you must increase its air intake by adding new cold-air returns. In the basement, this is relatively simple. Just place a grille at floor level and pipe it to the cold-air drop or return plenum on the furnace — the part that feeds cold air to the blower compartment. It's also a relatively simple operation to cut a return opening into the floor of a first-floor room and duct or pipe it to the return drop. You may prefer to place the return grille in a wall or partition. This is a little more difficult but well within the capabilities of most do-it-yourselfers.

First, pry away the shoe molding with a chisel or other tool. Find wall studs by tapping on the wall (a hollow sound indicates a wall cavity; a solid thump means a stud) or, if your ear is not that finely attuned, with a magnetic stud finder (the magnet does not react to the wood stud, of course, but to the nails that hold wallboard or lath to the stud). Check both in the room and in the basement to make sure that no wires are in the way — you don't want a shocking experience when you cut through the floor. Place the grille against the baseboard between studs, and mark the baseboard at the ends of the grille. Set the grille aside, and drill ¾-inch starter holes through the floor just inside the lines. With a keyhole saw, cut away the baseboard just inside the lines.

Mark on the wall 1 inch inside of the cutaway baseboard, up to 1 inch less than the

1. Pry away base shoe molding (right).

2. Locate stud by tapping (below left), or with a stud finder (below right).

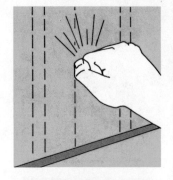

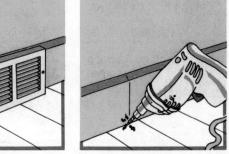

3. Mark baseboard for location of grille.

4. Drill starter holes through the floor.

5. Cut the baseboard away with a keyhole saw (right).

6. Mark wall inside the cutaway baseboard (far right).

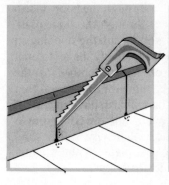
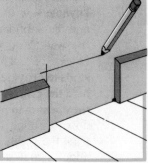

7. Drill starter holes through the floor.

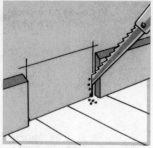

8. Cut away floor plate and wall.

9. You might have to nail blocks to studs (above).

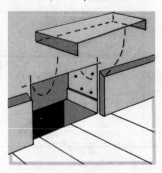

10. Cap off wall opening (above right).

11. Now you can attach the grille (right).

height of the grille, and mark a horizontal line at that point. Drill starter holes inside the lines at an angle through the floor. Use a keyhole saw to cut through the floor plate and the subfloor and to cut the opening in the wall. You will probably have to nail blocks of 2×4 or 1-inch lumber to the studs to provide backing for the screws that hold the grille. You will also have to cap off the opening to prevent air from being drawn down through the wall cavity rather than from the room. Cut a piece of sheet metal about 1 inch wider (4½ inches for a 2×4

wall) and 2 inches longer than the opening. Notch the back corners and bend down a 1-inch flange in the back and at each end. Insert into the wall opening, flush with the top, and nail through the end flanges into the studs or blocks. Then attach the grille. Cut the shoe molding to fit flush with the grille and nail it back in place.

In the basement, you can use the space between the joists below the new opening to duct the return air to the return drop or to a return line. Simply close off the joist space with hardboard or other material nailed across the bottom. At the duct, cut a hole in the top to admit the return air. Cap off the ends of the joist runs with sheet metal or wood headers to keep the system closed.

It is considerably more difficult to cut a return in an upper-floor room, although it can be done if there is no floor installed. Wall plates must be cut away to allow the passage of air, and caps installed between joists to direct the air where you want it to go. If a floor has already been put down, you may prefer to cut a return somewhere near the foot of the stairs on the first floor to draw the cooled air from upstairs and direct it to the furnace. While this may result in a drafty staircase, it is a compromise that generally does the job.

Basement connection of cold-air return.

COLD AIR RETURN DUCT

Closed returns are not as important with a gravity system. Chances are the existing returns will provide sufficient air to supply the new outlets. If not, a new return can be cut into the first floor as above.

EXTENDING A HOT-WATER SYSTEM

As with a warm-air system, the first consideration is the capacity of the system. If you are satisfied that it is up to the extra duty, it is not too difficult to tap into the piping.

On a one-pipe system, with a single main circling the basement and returning to the boiler, you can simply tap into the main to supply additional radiators or convectors on the first floor and above.

Copper pipe is generally used for hot-water systems. Decide where the main can best be tapped, as near to the new outlet as possible. Turn off the water at a shutoff valve somewhere behind the point to be tapped and, if possible, drain the line. (Unfortunately, drainage valves are not always located where you want them. In that case, you might drill a small hole at the point where the tap will be made and let the water trickle into a bucket, rather than come at you in a torrent when you cut through the line.)

Cut through the pipe with a hacksaw or tubing cutter, removing a section large enough to allow the insertion of a tee fitting of the same size as that used to feed other branches in the line. File off any burrs on the cut ends of the pipe. Clean the outside ends of the pipe and the inside of the tee with steel wool or emery cloth.

Copper pipe is assembled by "sweating" the joints—heating them and running in solder to seal and secure them. First apply a coat of soldering flux to both the pipe and the inside of the tee. Place the tee on the pipe and twist slightly to spread the flux

1. Drill a small hole into the pipe to drain the water.

2. Cut through the pipe with a hacksaw.

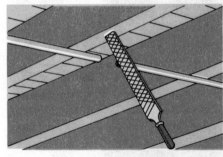

3. File off any burrs on the cut ends.

4. Clean ends with steel wool or emery cloth.

5. Apply flux.   6. Twist fitting to spread flux.

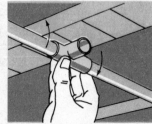

Heating a New or Remodeled Space ● Chapter 4

evenly. If you are sweating a joint near wood structural members, such as joists or subflooring, protect the wood from the flame of the propane torch by placing asbestos sheeting over the area. Heat the fitting at the joint until the flux begins to bubble out of the joint. Back off the torch and hold a strip of solder to the heated joint; it should flow around evenly and be drawn into the joint by capillary action. Wipe off excess solder and allow to harden—this should take less than a minute. Attach pipe and other fittings as necessary to reach the new radiator or convector. The pipe can simply be brought up through the floor to

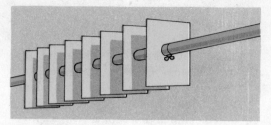

Aluminum fin clusters.

reach a first-floor outlet. For a second-floor outlet, you will have to drill a hole slightly larger than the pipe through the subflooring and floor plate, and another from the upper floor through the top plate, to allow the pipe to be brought up inside a first-floor partition. This may require lifting some floorboards on the second floor. Make sure you do this operation early in the framing stage of your project—it will be a lot easier then than as an afterthought.

A one-pipe system requires that the outlets be several inches above the main for proper functioning. For this reason, radiators or convectors are not usually practical for heating basement rooms in such a system. Aluminum fins can be installed in clusters over the main to radiate heat into a basement, however. They are fastened in place with sheet-metal screws, clamps, or tabs. If the room is finished, they can be concealed behind perforated sheet metal or similar material that will allow the passage of heat.

Tapping into a two-pipe system for additional outlets is done similarly, except that both supply and return lines must be provided. With this system, radiators or convectors need not be above the main line, so they can be used in the basement as well as the upper floors. The return outlet must be above the boiler water line, however, so the units must be installed high enough on the wall to allow this. Heat fins can also be used with this system—on the hot-water line, of course.

Extending a steam heating system is generally done the same way as with hot water. Because of the more exacting design re-

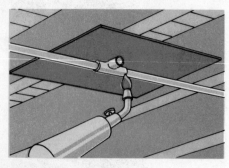

7. Apply heat with a torch.

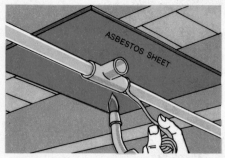

ASBESTOS SHEET

8. Hold solder to the heated joint.

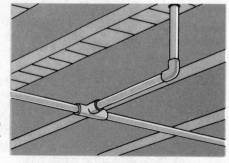

9. Bring pipe up to first-floor outlet.

quired of such a system, however, it is recommended that this work be left to a qualified contractor.

TIME FOR A CHANGE?

There is always the possibility that your present heating system, in the opinion of the experts and by your own reckoning, just isn't adequate to heat the new living space. If your present furnace is a monstrous relic with an insatiable thirst for fuel as it clanks and sputters its way through old age, this might well be the time to start from scratch with a modern, efficient unit that has enough capacity to heat the new rooms as well as the existing ones. You might also opt for a completely new ductwork system that will add considerably to basement headroom in addition to the space you will gain by replacing the old colossus with a compact modern furnace. Although this may seem like an expensive way out, you may be better off lumping all the expenses together, rather than having to replace the furnace in a few years anyway while living with less than satisfactory heating in the new room or rooms.

If the existing furnace is doing its job well, but simply can't be called upon for additional service, there are other solutions. One is to install a second, smaller furnace, with its own system of ductwork and pipes to heat the new area, and possibly even one or two adjacent rooms to take some of the load off the existing furnace. You can often find used furnaces in perfectly good condition, units that have been replaced by larger-capacity furnaces to serve the same purpose that you need to serve. But be wary. Buy such a unit only from a reputable contractor who will back it up with some kind of guarantee. Or, if you are thinking of buying a used furnace from an individual, have it checked out by an expert—your fuel oil dealer or a representative of the local utility—before you lay out the cash. Don't buy trouble.

Perhaps the simplest solution to heating your new room is an individual space heater. A gas heating unit installed in an outside wall can provide even, quiet heat for a room. Just make certain that it is vented to the outside. Never use an unvented gas heater; such an installation is extremely hazardous and is prohibited in many parts of the country. A properly vented heater is perfectly safe.

Electric baseboard heaters are another way to provide heat for the new room. Many types are available (see CHAPTER 1). Most come with specific installation instructions that should be diligently followed. Installed along outside walls, the electric units combine warm air with radiant heating. But before investing in electric baseboards, make sure that your electrical system has the capacity to accommodate them. Check with a licensed electrician or your utility company. If extensive rewiring is needed, you may be better off with some other type of heating.

FIREPLACES

A fireplace is not really intended as a primary source of heat in a room. In fact, it can actually cause a heat loss if there is a considerable difference between indoor and outdoor temperatures. A fire in the fireplace generates a considerable flow of air up through the chimney. The source of this air is generally the furnace-heated air in the rest of the house. With a properly designed and dampered chimney, however, this need not be the case, and a fireplace can be a good source of supplemental heat in the new room. In milder climates, where it is only necessary to "take the chill off" at night, a fireplace may handle the job more

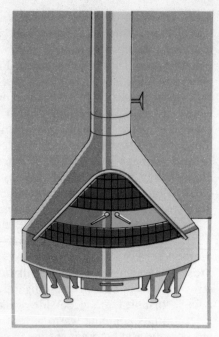

Freestanding prefabricated fireplace.

Prefabricated in-wall fireplace.

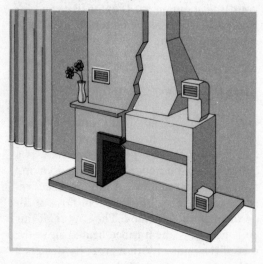

than adequately. And, of course, there is the psychological warmth of that crackling fire and the glowing embers.

You are not likely to find a masonry fireplace built into an attic, basement, or garage that you are finishing, although you may want to plan such a unit as an integral part of a new addition. But it is not difficult to install a modern, freestanding, prefabricated fireplace. These come in all sizes, shapes, and colors, in both wood-burning and realistic "gas-log" models. Some units are also available for building into a wall. These have the appearance of a conventional fireplace but do not require the heavy concrete foundation of a masonry unit. They can be framed in with wood or any other common building material.

A prefab fireplace can sometimes be vented through the existing chimney, but check local building codes and a competent engineer on this point. You can also install a prefabricated chimney, but again check local ordinances, which often set restrictions on use of certain types of chimney materials.

Installation of a prefabricated fireplace and chimney is a job that requires no special skills beyond those of most home handymen. The chimney must be run above the roof to the height dictated by the local code, usually a minimum of 2 feet above the ridge, or 3 feet above a flat roof. If working at heights—even the height of a ranch house roof—is not for you, hire a contractor. Otherwise, you can do the entire project yourself. Just how it is done will depend on the type of fireplace and chimney you select. Again, follow manufacturer's directions to the letter.

5

Routine Maintenance and Servicing

A MODERN heating system is quite a mechanical marvel. But, as with all marvelous mechanisms, things can sometimes go wrong. When they do, you may be able to set them right yourself, but if it's more than a simple fixit, you will probably be better off calling in a qualified serviceman.

If you heat with oil and have a delivery contract, you may also have a service contract to cover emergencies and, possibly, annual checkups and maintenance as well. Most gas utilities have emergency crews ready to cope with problems. If such services are not available in your area, have the name and phone number of a competent service contractor noted near your telephone. If electricity provides your heat, find a good electrician. It is wise to have these professionals in to check over your system even if nothing is wrong. It will be money well spent—they will know something about your heating system and, more important, they will know you. You won't just be some stranger calling on them to come out in the middle of a cold, snowy night to turn your heat back on.

Of course, it is better to avoid having to call on them at all. The "ounce of prevention" will lessen the likelihood of emergencies arising. That ounce is in the form of routine maintenance, most of which you *can* do yourself.

ROUTINE MAINTENANCE

A forced-air heating system sends out hot air to the rooms of the house and draws cooled air back to be reheated and recirculated. It also draws back household dirt, dust, and lint. To prevent these impurities from being recirculated as well, one or more filters are located either in the cold-air drop or inside the blower compartment. By the very nature of their work, these filters will become clogged if they are not regularly maintained. If this is allowed to happen, the cooled air will not pass through into the furnace heat exchanger, and the system will become "starved" for air. Uneven and certainly unsatisfactory heating will be the result, as well as an unnecessarily high consumption of fuel.

Air filters should be cleaned or replaced every 30 to 60 days during the heating season. The most common type are disposable, costing a few dollars at most. You can check them by taking them out of their compartments and holding them up to a light; if little or no light shines through, they are past due for replacement. If a disposable filter appears to have more useful life in it, you can vacuum-clean it, or tap it, intake side down, onto newspapers spread on the floor to remove most of the accumulated dirt. Then reposition it until time for replacement. Arrows on the edges of the filter indicate the direction of air flow. It is important that this positioning be observed;

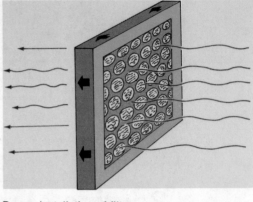
Proper installation of filter.

otherwise the filter will quickly become clogged.

Somewhat more expensive are cleanable filters, but the extra cost is offset by the considerably longer life of the filter. These should be checked frequently just like the disposable variety, and vacuum-cleaned or washed with soap and water, following manufacturer's directions for the particular type.

Dirt can interfere with your forced-air heating system in other ways as well. Clean the fan blade or blower that moves the air at least once a year. It tends to accumulate dirt that might pass through the filter (especially if the filter itself is allowed to become dirty) or be drawn through the

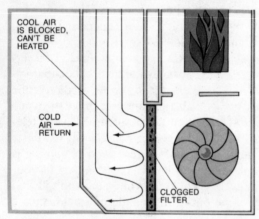

COOL AIR IS BLOCKED, CAN'T BE HEATED

COLD AIR RETURN

CLOGGED FILTER

Clogged filter.

Check for dirt.   Vacuum clean filter.   Tap out dirt.

Chapter 5 ● Routine Maintenance and Servicing

Clean the blower.

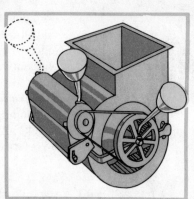

Oil the blower.

Check belt tension.

openings around the blower compartment door. To function properly, it must be clean.

While you are cleaning the blower and its compartment, oil the blower and motor ports (unless they have sealed bearings). A few drops are usually sufficient—don't over-lubricate. On belt-drive blowers, check belt tension at the same time. It should deflect easily but not sloppily as you squeeze it gently. If a belt is too taut, it will cause undue wear. A too-loose belt may lead to slippage, also causing wear and possibly damage to the motor, as well as erratic operation of the fan.

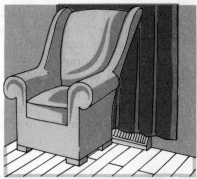

Keep registers and grilles clear of furniture and other obstructions.

Registers and diffusers should be vacuum-cleaned every few weeks, along with return grilles. This applies to gravity as well as forced-air systems. Make sure there is a clear path for warm air coming out of the registers, unobstructed by curtains or furniture.

With a hot-water system, you must bleed the air from the lines periodically. With time, a certain amount of air will find its way into the pipes in the system, eventually settling in the radiators at the upper levels of the house. Where there is air, it keeps out the hot water. There is usually a small valve at the top of each radiator. At least once a year, or more often if a radiator seems to

Clean registers.

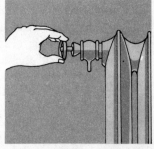

Bleed radiators.

have trouble heating up, hold a bucket under this valve and open it, keeping it open until water starts to flow out. Be careful—that water will be hot! Shut the valve when the water flows steadily without sputtering.

Other routine maintenance on a hot-water system is usually best left to a profes-

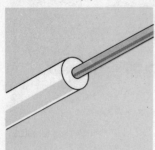

Insulate steam pipes.

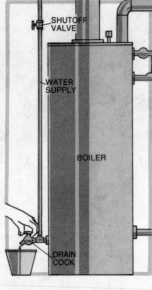

Drain boiler.

SHUTOFF VALVE

WATER SUPPLY

BOILER

DRAIN COCK

sional serviceman. Once a year, usually shortly before the heating season begins, have him check the pump operation, check the operation of the flow control valve, check for piping leaks and valve operation, oil the pump motor, and drain and flush the boiler. On most systems, you can probably perform this last operation yourself—ask the serviceman to show you how.

With steam heat, have the serviceman give the system an annual checkup. You can help the system by insulating steam pipes that run through areas you don't want to heat. Every two to three weeks during the heating season, open the valve at the bottom of the boiler and drain off a bucket of water. This will keep sediment from settling on the bottom of the boiler. Sediment that is allowed to remain there will actually insulate the boiler from the flame in the burner and result in a lot of heat (and fuel dollars) going up the chimney rather than being converted into comfort for your home.

BURNER CARE

An oil burner should be checked by the serviceman every year to insure clean, satisfactory, economical (as much as possible in these days when no fuel is really eco-

nomical) heat. Have him clean the burner and adjust the fuel-to-air ratio for maximum efficiency. He should clean the heating elements and surfaces and make sure that there are no oil leaks. Oil filters and the burner nozzle should be changed, and the oil pump checked. And make sure he checks all electrical connections, especially on safety devices.

There are several tests that you might ask the serviceman to perform to check on the oil furnace's efficiency. A draft test will indicate whether excessive heat is being lost up the chimney or if there is insufficient draft for proper combustion of the oil. A smoke test will show whether the oil is being burned cleanly and completely. A CO_2 test will also show how completely your oil (and your dollars) are being burned. A stack temperature test will show if stack gases are too hot or not hot enough for efficiency as well as safety. All these tests require the use of special equipment; make sure that your serviceman has such equipment and uses it.

A gas furnace (bottled, LP, or natural) requires less frequent maintenance—every three years should do it. Have the serviceman check the operation of the main gas valve, the pressure regulator, and the safety control valve. The primary air supply nozzle should be adjusted for proper combustion. A draft test and stack temperature test, as described for oil furnaces, should also be performed.

If you heat with coal, adjust and clean the stoker at the end of each heating season, following the manufacturer's directions. Clean the burner of all coal, ash, and clinkers (a messy but necessary job). Oil the inside of the coal screw and hopper to prevent rust.

With an electric furnace, very little maintenance is required. Check the manufacturer's directions that came with the unit, and follow those recommendations.

When the serviceman tells you (as he inevitably will) that major repairs are required, you will face the question of whether to repair or replace. Get several estimates on both courses—the larger the job, the more estimates. Check around with friends and neighbors to compare heating costs. If yours seem to be far above the norm, it may be time to scrap the old and start anew. When you have narrowed your choice of contractors, ask each one how many years he thinks it will take before the amount you save by having the new system equals what you will have to pay for it. Bear in mind that fuel costs will almost surely continue to go up—doesn't everything? Then weigh all these factors and make your decision.

HEATING PROBLEMS

You may first perceive it as a noticeable chill while you are viewing a hot cops-and-robbers chase on television, or when you get out of bed some frigid morning with icicles forming on every breath you take. You glance at the thermostat—it is set for 65 degrees, but the temperature is in the low 40's. The furnace is out! Your first impulse might be to chuck it all and migrate to the perpetual warmth of Pago Pago. Or you might consider a more practical, if far less appealing, solution like moving the family into the cozy confines of your mother-in-law's house "for the duration." As you button up your overcoat and chug-a-lug a cup of steaming coffee, it probably occurs to you that you should call the serviceman. But before you put those numbed fingers to work dialing the telephone, wait . . .

First check the main burner switch. If the furnace is in the basement, the switch may be located on the staircase wall. It is not uncommon for a person to brush against it while carrying a load of laundry up or down the steps, shutting off the system. If the

house is warm and the weather outside not too blustery cold, it may be some time before the furnace stoppage is noted. Make sure the switch is on, then make sure that the fuse or circuit breaker that services the furnace line is not blown or tripped. If necessary, replace the fuse with one of the same rating, or reset the breaker. If the circuit again blows, the problem is electrical. Call the serviceman.

If that checks out, consider the fuel supply. If you heat with oil, look at the gauge on top of the oil tank, or wherever it is located if you have an underground tank. Should the gauge read Empty or close to it, call your dealer for an immediate refill. If coal supplies your heat, a quick glance at the bin will tell you if you are out—and you have no one to blame but yourself. The same is true of bottled gas. If gas for your furnace is piped in, that should not be a problem unless there is a severe gas shortage in your area—and then you should hear about it through the news media. You may

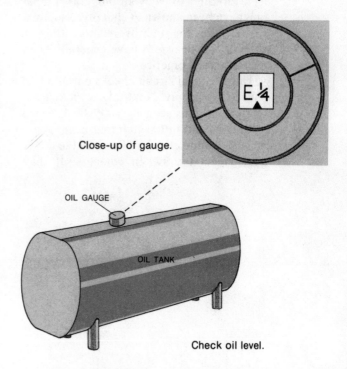

Close-up of gauge.

OIL GAUGE

OIL TANK

Check oil level.

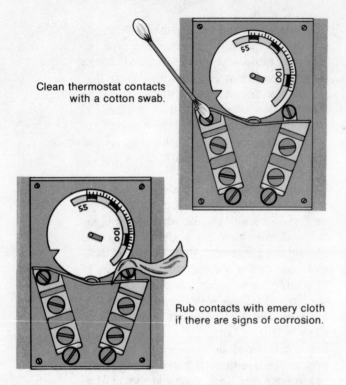

Clean thermostat contacts with a cotton swab.

Rub contacts with emery cloth if there are signs of corrosion.

look dirty, clean them with a cotton swab dipped in alcohol. If there are any signs of corrosion, rub the contacts with a piece of very fine emery cloth. Turn the thermostat to its highest setting to see if the furnace burner comes on. If not, it's probably time to call the serviceman (hopefully, those fingers of yours are still operative and not frostbitten by this time).

Not all furnace problems are signaled by a total shutdown. Some that are scarcely noticeable at first may be harbingers of troubles to come. A burner that incessantly repeats the on-off cycle may indicate a clogged filter. If your inspection acquits the filter, call in the serviceman. A blower that just won't quit when it should could be another indication of a clogged filter, or it could mean that the return grilles are blocked by furniture or some other obstacles. Check out these possibilities before calling for help.

A noisy blower might be quieted by tightening the blades or correcting the belt tension. Or it may be thirsty for oil. But if you can't spot an obvious cause, call the serviceman. If you smell gas or a combustion odor, immediately shut down the heating system and call the utility or oil company. The message should be clear—other than for regular maintenance and simple repairs, the heating system is not really amateur territory. But you sure have to know what to expect from it and from the professionals on whom you call for help.

have forgotten to pay your bill. Gas companies have been known to shut off residential fuel supplies for such oversights, although recent court decisions have generally been averse to such practices.

The electrical circuit checks out and you have a fuel supply. Next take a look at the thermostat. This seemingly mystical device is simply a form of switch that is activated by temperature changes. Remove the cover and inspect the switch contacts. If they

6

Keeping Cool

MAN HAS BEEN looking for ways to keep cool for almost as long as he has been seeking warmth. The picture of Cleopatra lounging in her barge surrounded by slaves waving huge fans to waft the cooling breezes of the Nile in her direction is a familiar one. And, indeed, it was an effective method of air conditioning – for Cleopatra, if not for the slaves.

But it has only been over the past 20 or so years that air conditioners as we know them today have come into widespread popularity. If summer daytime temperatures in your region normally rise to the 80's or above, you probably think of an air conditioner as a necessity rather than the luxury it was considered a few decades ago. It is somewhat ironic that the power shortages that have become commonplace in recent years are felt most acutely in the hottest weather, caused by the use of air conditioners when they are most needed and resulting (sometimes) in the shutting down of those very cooling units. But we can hope that solutions will be found for these problems and that hot-weather comfort will continue to be a pleasant reality.

Of course, in many regions an air conditioner is not really needed. There are other alternatives to cool a home. You may be able to reach an acceptable warm-weather comfort level by installing an exhaust fan in the attic to remove hot air and circulate cooler air through the house. Adding, or improving, insulation is another help to year-round comfort. Installing an awning or planting trees to block out heat-causing sunlight is effective, especially where excessive heat and humidity are only an occasional problem. Even if you do opt for air conditioning, these steps should be taken to help you get the most out of the unit you choose.

BENEFITS OF AIR CONDITIONING

The benefits of air conditioning are many. In addition to lowering temperatures inside the home, an air conditioner reduces the humidity level that causes the "clammy" hot-weather discomfort. It also removes dust and pollen from the air, providing a more healthful and comfortable environment for the family. On somewhat cooler days when heat isn't a problem, the unit can be used to circulate air throughout the room or the entire house, or to exhaust smoke, odors, or stale air.

There are various methods of air condi-

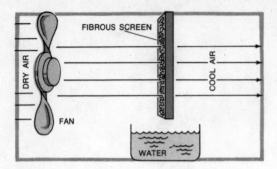

Cooling by evaporation.

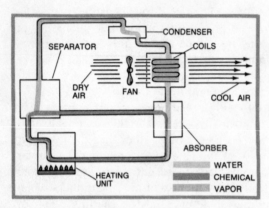

Cooling by absorption.

the coils. A fan blows air passing over the coils throughout the house. Such a system is fairly effective but quite unwieldy and expensive for home installations.

By far the most common and popular type of air conditioning for today's homes is a refrigerated unit.

HOW REFRIGERATED AIR CONDITIONING WORKS

In its simplest form, an air conditioner is a heat-transfer mechanism. It removes heat from where it is not wanted (indoors) and disposes of it at a convenient location (outdoors). Basically, an air conditioner, a refrigerator, and a home freezer all operate on the same principle and use equipment that is closely related.

A complete air-conditioning system, whether it is a small window unit or a large central unit, includes an evaporator or cooling coil, a compressor, a condenser coil, a capillary tube, a blower fan for circulating air, and a power unit for operating the compresser and blower. Since air conditioners work on the principle of removing heat, a refrigerant is needed. The refrigerant or coolant is Freon, a chemical that boils at

tioning. Cooling by evaporation is probably the simplest and oldest. Air cooled by evaporated water is circulated by a fan. However, this type of cooling is satisfactory only in very dry areas—otherwise the cooled air is likely to be damp and muggy, perhaps making you feel even more uncomfortable than without such a system.

An absorption system of cooling works somewhat like a coffee percolator, heating a mixture of water and chemicals so that it rises from the bottom to the top of the system. Here, the coolant fluid is separated and the chemicals flow back to an absorber, where they are cooled. The water rises as a vapor to the highest point in the system, where it enters a condenser and is cooled to return to liquid state. It then flows over cooling coils in a vacuum system that causes it to become a vapor again, chilling

Refrigerated cooling.

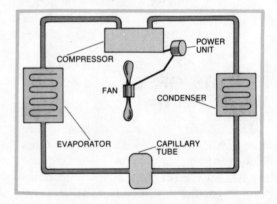

COOLING COIL

BLOWER

MOTOR

FILTER

AIR RETURN DUCT

FAN

MOTOR

COIL

COMPRESSOR

DRAIN PIPE

Split central air-conditioning system (compressor and condenser coils are outside the house).

from 20 to 40 degrees below zero. Normally, Freon is a gas, but when stored under pressure in a tightly sealed chamber, it becomes a liquid. When pressure is released suddenly, the Freon begins to boil, and the evaporation taking place inside the chamber causes the sides of the container to become "ice" cold. If the evaporation takes place inside a coil and the coil is exposed to warm room air, the intense cold begins absorbing the heat from the air.

The components of an air conditioner work together to absorb heat inside an area. The blower fan draws warm air from the room and passes it over the evaporator coils on the inside, cooling the air, and then returns it to the room. Dehumidifying the air takes place when the moisture in the warm air begins cooling. The moisture left on the evaporator or cooling coils is eventually picked up by the fan and vaporized. The result is not only cooler air, but drier air. Before the cooled air from the evaporator is passed back into the room, it goes through a filter that removes dirt, pollen, dust, and other undesirable foreign matter.

Since the Freon must be used over and over again, it is cycled through a compres-

sor. This works like a pump, compressing the Freon gas, thereby raising its temperature to about 210 degrees. The hot gas is then routed outside to the condenser coils, where it is cooled by outside air and the blower fan. Once the heat is removed from the compressed gas, it turns to a liquid state and is ready to begin the same cycle again.

The compressed gas is further aided in the cycle by flowing through a capillary tube of much smaller size than the coil. The restriction in the capillary tube meters the Freon in its flow to the evaporator.

Armed with basic knowledge of how an air conditioner functions, the next step is to determine the type that suits your needs. There are many brands on the market today, and each manufacturer offers a number of models, types, and installation variations.

CENTRAL AIR CONDITIONERS

Central air conditioners are usually year-round units, cooling the house in the summer and heating in winter. These units have the compressor and condenser coils outside the house and the evaporator coils and heating unit inside. A central unit is usually connected with a duct system (like a warm-air heating system) to distribute the air uniformly throughout the house.

The most popular form of central air conditioning is called a split system. It is designed to work in conjunction with existing warm-air furnaces using the present ductwork and furnace blower as integral parts of the cooling system, serving as the air distribution network. The condensing unit for the system often sits on an outdoor cement slab adjacent to the house, but it can also be placed in the garage, on the roof, in the remote recesses of the yard, or even in the wall of the home.

A thermostat is conveniently located inside to control temperatures. You can set the temperature during both summer and winter for total comfort. A simple switch changes it from cooling to heating.

Cooling coils absorb heat and excessive moisture from the air that is circulating through the duct system of your home. The cooled air is then recirculated throughout the house. The cooling coils can be readily adapted to forced-air heating units presently using an upflow furnace, downflow furnace, or horizontal furnace.

Central air conditioning can also be adapted for use with steam, hot water, or central electric heating systems. If your home is heated with any of these, however, ductwork must be installed to distribute cool air throughout the house.

A central air conditioning system will provide even temperatures for your family twelve months of the year. Hot spots or cold spots are eliminated with a properly installed system. Humidity is kept at a constant level, making for less frequent colds and relief for sinus sufferers. Airborne dust and dirt are also greatly reduced, keeping the entire house cleaner.

Although central air conditioning might sound like the greatest thing since sliced bread, it does have some shortcomings, primarily economic. The cost of a central system can run high, especially if ductwork must be added. The ideal time to install this system is when the house is in the construction stage. The installation is not for amateurs, but rather for qualified contractors. Homes located in regions with mild climates would not reap the full benefits of central air conditioning.

ROOM AIR CONDITIONING

For most homeowners, there are many advantages to installing a room air conditioner rather than a central air-conditioning system. A central system may be excessively expensive to install if you live in an older house, or unnecessarily expensive in a climate where air conditioning is needed only occasionally for short periods. Window air-conditioning units have become common in households across the country because of their compact styling, portability, and ease of installation. Another important advantage is the substantially lower cost of maintenance. Window units can be installed in one or two rooms, or in the case of modern, lightweight models, moved from room to room wherever they are needed.

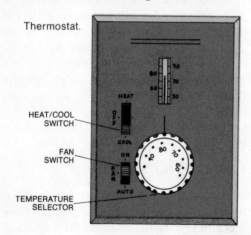

Thermostat.

HEAT/COOL SWITCH

FAN SWITCH

TEMPERATURE SELECTOR

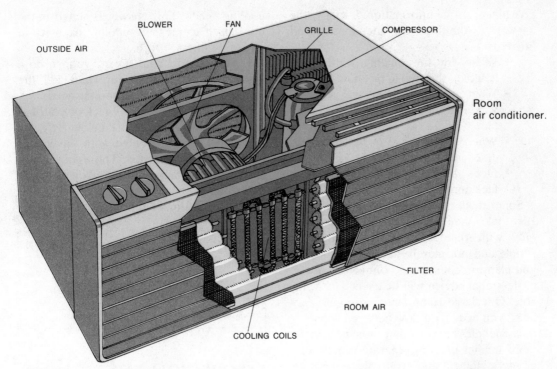

BLOWER   FAN   GRILLE   COMPRESSOR

OUTSIDE AIR

Room
air conditioner.

FILTER

ROOM AIR

COOLING COILS

Although room air conditioners differ in cabinet styling, weight, and component placement, they all basically function the same way, performing four jobs to make you comfortable on a hot, humid day. They cool the air, remove moisture from the air, filter out dust, and circulate the air inside a room or several rooms.

The operation of a room air conditioner is basically the same as a central unit. Although smaller, the components are much the same and do the same jobs. The evaporator section of the room unit projects into the room, and the condenser-compressor compartment extends to the outside of the house.

ESTIMATING COOLING NEEDS

Before you select a room air conditioner for your home, it is important to determine the cooling capacity needed. If the cooling

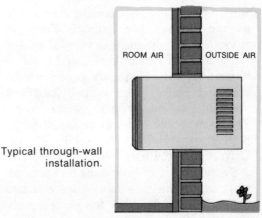

ROOM AIR   OUTSIDE AIR

Typical through-wall
installation.

capacity of a unit is too small for the room where you plan to use it, it will not do an adequate job of cooling and dehumidifying. If it is too large for the room, it will probably cost more and not dehumidify properly. You can arrive at a cooling capacity estimate in several ways.

A salesman at a reputable air conditioner dealer can make an estimate for you if you give him accurate information. Usually, the answers to the following questions are all he needs:

- What are the height, width, and length of the area to be cooled?
- What are the number and sizes of windows and the directions they face?
- Where is the space to be cooled located in the house?
- Does the longest side of the room face north, east, south, or west?

Some dealers offer free home surveys. Just make sure, as always, that you deal only with reputable and knowledgeable people and not merely hard-sell artists. If you plan to cool several connected rooms, professional advice will be especially valuable. One large room air conditioner may be all you need if air flow between rooms is free enough, but in other homes two or more smaller units in separate rooms may be more efficient and economical. Another way to determine your cooling needs is to use the Cooling Load Estimate Form for Room Air Conditioners developed by the Association of Home Appliance Manufacturers (AHAM). If you are good with figures and prefer doing such calculations yourself, you may wish to go this route. The form is free and can be obtained by writing to AHAM, 20 North Wacker Drive, Chicago, Illinois 60606.

If you don't care to be quite that precise, you can make a reasonably good estimate of your cooling needs by following a fairly simple method. Find the volume of the room by multiplying the width, length, and height in feet. Multiply this number by 10 if the roof or attic is well insulated or if another room is above. If the room has many windows or an uninsulated roof, multiply instead by 18. Now multiply by 16 if the longest wall faces north, by 17 if it faces east, by 18 if it faces south, by 19 if it faces west. Divide this result by 60 to find your

cooling needs. This answer is stated in the units used to measure cooling capacity in air conditioners: Btu/h.

If you plan to cool several rooms, do a calculation for each room, then add the answers to find your total cooling needs.

You can make a quick check of your figures by consulting the list below. It compares space to be cooled with "average" cooling capacity needed. These, of course, are "ballpark" figures, since other variables enter into your calculations, but they will give an indication of approximate needs.

Space to be cooled	Cooling needed (Btu/h)
medium-size bedroom	5,000–6,000
medium-size living room	8,000–12,000
several connected rooms	15,000–20,000
medium-size house	24,000 or more

BEFORE YOU BUY

Room air conditioners come in a number of styles. One consideration is whether a unit is to be mounted in a window or through a wall. Some models are sold with adapters and can be mounted in several ways.

If a unit is to be window-mounted, its shape and dimensions will be determined by the shape and dimensions of the window. If the unit doesn't fit properly, an airtight installation is difficult to achieve. If you don't have an airtight installation, the conditioner will never cool up to its capacity.

Double-hung windows, in which the sash slides up and down, accept conventional air conditioners that are box-shaped and wider than they are high. When such a unit is installed, the bottom sash rests on the top of the conditioner. Panels supplied with the air conditioner fill in side spaces.

Casement windows, which swing out and

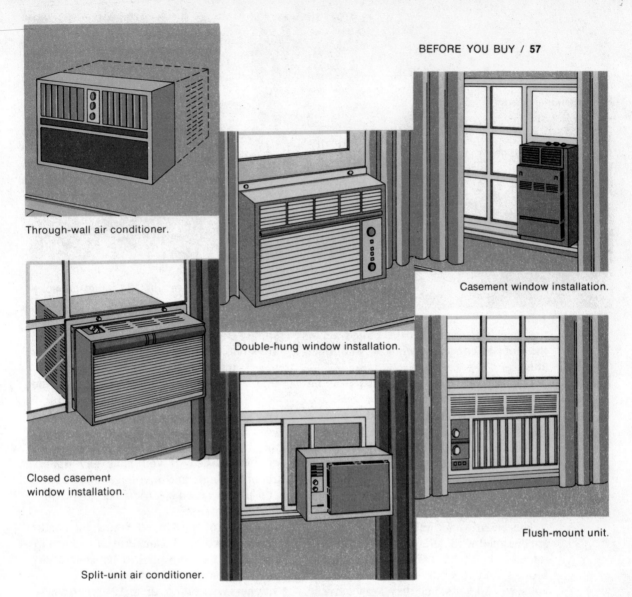

Through-wall air conditioner.

Double-hung window installation.

Casement window installation.

Closed casement window installation.

Flush-mount unit.

Split-unit air conditioner.

in like a door, and windows that slide horizontally usually require tall, narrow conditioners. Such conditioners are installed in windows left completely or partly open; fit of these is critical.

For closed casement windows, a specially shaped conditioner is available that has a small front and is deep from front to back. It is installed by removing one or two small panes of glass and inserting the unit in the opening.

For both sash and sliding windows, U-shaped, split-unit conditioners are also available. This type allows installation with a minimum of open window space that must be sealed by panels or other devices.

In some areas local laws or building regulations require that a conditioner must not project more than a certain distance from the outside of a building wall. Check to see if such rules apply to your home. If they do, ask your dealer about air conditioners designed with a minimal overhang.

Another special type fits almost flush with the window in which it is placed. You may consider this type of unit more attrac-

Poor interior location.

Poor exterior location.

tive because drapes can be pulled across the front to conceal it when it is not operating.

Location of the air conditioner is an important consideration. A window that faces north is best because it is shaded most of the day. The unit should not be installed in a window where outdoor airflow will be blocked by a nearby building or dense bushes. Inside, avoid room corners or places where large pieces of furniture could hinder air circulation.

The electric motors in air conditioners are designed with different volt and ampere ratings to fit different home wiring systems. Motors may operate on 115 volts, 210 volts, or 230 volts, and they draw currents ranging from less than 7.5 to over 25 amperes

To find the conditioner best suited for your home, you must know the electrical capacity of your wiring in volts and amperes, the codes in your area with regard to connecting air conditioners to home wiring, and the electrical load on the wiring. A conditioner that draws more current than the wiring will safely carry can cause blown fuses or a fire hazard. If your wiring is inadequate for the conditioner you want to buy, you have only two choices: buy a smaller

air conditioner or install higher-capacity wiring in your home.

Circuits in most homes and apartments supply electricity at about 115 volts and 15 amperes. Kitchens and laundry rooms may have circuits that supply 20 amperes. Before you buy a conditioner, find out the amperage of the outlet where the unit will be located. One way to do this is to check your house or apartment fuse box and read the amperes from the appropriate fuse or circuit breaker. If you have any doubts about the amperage or voltage of the outlet, consult a licensed electrician or public utility representative.

In most of the United States, air conditioners that draw 7.5 amperes or less at 115 volts may be connected to household circuits. In some areas and buildings, air conditioners with ratings up to 12 amperes may be plugged into 115-volt, single-outlet circuits, but nowhere should units drawing more than 12 amperes be connected to 15-ampere, 115-volt circuits. Few houses or apartments are equipped with single-outlet, 115-volt circuits. Installing them should be left to a licensed electrician and can cost anywhere from $25 to $125, depending on the capacity of the existing building wiring and the location of the outlet. Only if you have considerable wiring experience should you attempt the job yourself. Some localities require that only a licensed electrician do such work, or at least that all work be inspected by a licensed electrician—a good idea in any case.

To find the electrical rating allowable for a conditioner connected to your home wiring, contact the city or county engineer's office, a licensed electrician, or the electric utility company. You can also consult a local air conditioner dealer. Some offer a free home survey to determine any electrical changes that should be made to install various air conditioners. Again, consult only a reputable dealer.

If you live in an apartment, check with the building manager before you purchase a room air conditioner. Many buildings have strict rules about the maximum amperage allowed for air conditioners.

Even if you follow your local electrical code to the letter, it is possible to overload a circuit's current-carrying capacity if you plug other appliances into it in addition to the air conditioner. The combined load would result in tripped breakers or blown fuses, or even an electrical fire if the circuit is improperly wired or fused. To avoid this situation you must determine the circuit's load. You can check the load yourself if you know all the appliances and lights that are already on the circuit to which you plan to connect the air conditioner. Add the wattages of the appliances and the lights usually functioning and divide by 115 volts. The answer is the ampere load on the circuit without the conditioner. Then add the ampere rating of the conditioner to get your projected total load.

If the total is more than 12 amperes on a 15-ampere circuit, or more than 16 amperes on a 20-ampere circuit, you should install the conditioner on a circuit with fewer appliances or buy two small-amperage conditioners rather than one large one and put them on two different circuits. Another alternative is to have an electrician install another circuit.

If you are considering buying a 210- or 230-volt air conditioner, consult a qualified electrician or the local power company about the actual voltage delivered to your home. It may be anywhere from less than 200 volts to more than 240 volts.

SHOPPING FOR A ROOM AIR CONDITIONER

When shopping for an air conditioner, compare the efficiency of the units you are considering. With the spiraling costs of energy today, operating costs of the unit are a point to be reckoned with before laying out your hard-earned money. An air conditioner that operates more efficiently uses less electricity.

The initials EER stand for Energy Efficiency Ratio, something to check very closely when selecting an air conditioner. A unit's EER is computed by dividing the Btu/h by the watts of power used (both stated on a plate on the machine). The higher the resulting figure, the more efficient the air conditioner. The EER does not relate to cooling capacity, only efficiency. Two units with different EERs can provide an equal cooling capacity. Both will cool the room satisfactorily, but in so doing one will use less electricity. A conditioner that achieves an EER rating of 8 to 9 will ease your electric bills substantially during its lifetime.

There are certain practical and convenience features to look for in a room air conditioner. In this respect, shop for an air conditioner much the same as any appliance and treat your purchase as the investment it is.

Check to make sure the unit has been properly certified. A seal of approval, such as that of Underwriters' Laboratories, Inc., should be attached guaranteeing that it has

AHAM certification.

Seal of the
Underwriters' Laboratories.

BTU hr COOLING CAPACITY
AMPERES and WATTS RATING

AHAM
CERTIFIED

ASSOCIATION OF HOME
APPLIANCE MANUFACTURERS'
Room Air Conditioner Standard CN 1

FILTER

Removal of filter.

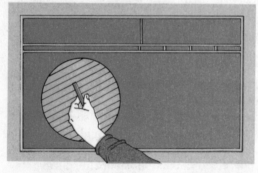

Adjusting the front grille to direct air flow.

met certain standards of electrical safety. Ratings for amperes, watts, and Btu/h should be indicated and a seal attached saying "AHAM-certified."

The warranty should state clearly how many years of free repair parts and labor you are buying with the unit. Be sure the warranty will be honored at a local authorized service shop. Check to see if additional in-home service contracts are available.

The unit's filter should be easy to remove and reinstall and either simple to clean or inexpensive to replace. Have the dealer demonstrate filter care.

The front of the unit should be both practical and good-looking. The front grille should be adjustable to direct air flow to the desired area. The grille "cleanability" should also be considered. Common features on a typical air conditioner include a thermostat to regulate room temperature, fan settings for additional cooling, and opening vents for bringing outside air into a room. Some models also feature heat controls for regulating heat on cool days, or fan-only settings to circulate fresh air. Have the dealer explain and demonstrate the use of all controls.

As with any major purchase, shop around. Consider the dealer's reputation in the community, experience in the business, and ability to deliver, install, and service what he sells. Friends, neighbors, or your local Better Business Bureau can possibly advise you.

Unit controls.

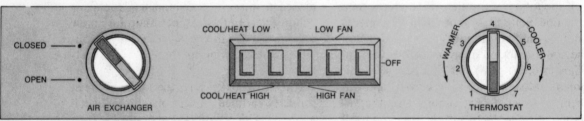

CLOSED
OPEN
AIR EXCHANGER

COOL/HEAT LOW   LOW FAN
OFF
COOL/HEAT HIGH   HIGH FAN

WARMER   4   COOLER
3   5
2   6
1   7
THERMOSTAT

AIR EXCHANGER CONTROL   **MASTER CONTROL**   **THERMOSTAT CONTROL**

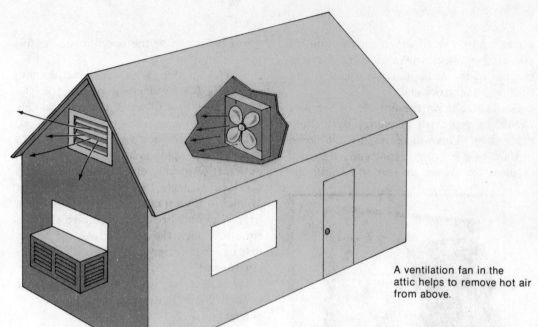

A ventilation fan in the attic helps to remove hot air from above.

Collect as much literature on the product as you can, and study it carefully, comparing different styles and models. Take your time and consider all possibilities before you reach for your wallet.

ROUTINE MAINTENANCE AND SIMPLE REPAIRS

Proper care and usage will greatly increase your satisfaction and the cooling you get from your room air conditioner, not to mention prolong its life. The best guide to a unit's use and care is your owner's manual. Keep it handy and consult it often.

The thermostat should generally be left alone once you have found a comfortable temperature. However, you should set the thermostat at a slightly higher temperature if you plan to be away for several hours. The reverse is true if you are entertaining a number of guests. People generate heat, so

the thermostat will probably need to be set at a slightly lower temperature.

Grilles should be adjusted so that cool air flows up, out, and away from the nearest wall to blanket the whole room. Fans should be set at high speed in hot weather to take full advantage of the conditioner's cooling capacity. During periods of cool, moist weather, low speed should be used for less cooling and more moisture removal.

The workload of your air conditioner will be greatly reduced if all windows and doors in the room to be cooled are kept closed. Shades or drapes should be pulled across the windows during the day. A ventilation fan in the attic to remove hot air from above will also help.

Cleaning and protection of certain conditioner parts are necessary occasionally to insure efficient, trouble-free cooling and to prevent service calls and repairs. Be sure to unplug the conditioner before performing any maintenance chores.

The filter should be cleaned or changed at least once a month to prevent dirt from collecting on the cooling coils and decreasing cooling efficiency. If the filter is reusable, it can be removed, washed in soap and water, and replaced damp on the unit. If you change filters, make sure the replacement is of the same material, quality, and thickness as the original.

Cooling coils on the outside of the unit should be protected in winter by a dustproof cover. This will keep out wind-blown dirt and help prevent rusting caused by rain or snow conditions. Be sure to remove the

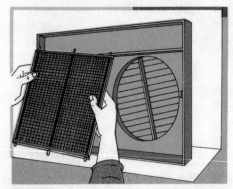

Installation of a new filter.

Protect outside coils in winter with a dustproof cover.

Vacuum clean the cooling coils.

cover before using the conditioner the following summer.

When something goes wrong, be sure you really need a serviceman before you call him. Check first to see if there is a simple solution.

If the conditioner won't run, check to make sure the plug is firmly in its electrical outlet. It's not only embarrassing to have a serviceman jiggle the cord to solve your problem—it's expensive. A blown fuse or a tripped circuit breaker could also cause a shutoff. Check these and replace a blown fuse or reset a tripped breaker. If the problem repeats, call the serviceman.

When a conditioner does not provide enough cooling, it sometimes indicates a clogged or dirty filter. Clean or replace the filter and vacuum-clean the cooling coils. Check the vents and window mounting to be sure no cool air is escaping.

If the unit still doesn't cool the room properly, call the local electric utility company to find out if there is temporary low voltage in your area. If there is, the efficiency of your conditioner may be lessened until voltage returns to normal. In this case a repairman would not be able to help. You might be better off shutting down the unit and suffering through the heat, rather than having it operate at the reduced voltage, which could damage the mechanism. Outside temperature can play tricks with your conditioner, too. If it is less than 70 degrees outside, water can drip inside the room. The solution to this problem is either to turn the unit completely off or to use the fan-only setting.

It takes some careful thought and planning to design an air-conditioning system perfect for your personal needs. And it takes proper care and maintenance to keep it keeping you cool. But it's worth a little sweat to save a lot, as you will appreciate when you are relaxing inside your cool house during the dog days of summer.

7

How to Save on Home Comfort Conditioning

Homeowners around the country are faced with a serious problem—conserving energy and money without sacrificing on comfort in the home. Although the problem is serious, the solutions are fairly simple. There are several energy-saving steps the average do-it-yourselfer can take without having a garage full of tools or laying out big bucks.

We all know that heating and cooling the home is taking a bigger and bigger bite out of the personal budget each year, and it probably won't get better. A few energy conservation steps can ease those monthly bills as well as add resale value to the home. With the dwindling natural resources of our country, the nation as a whole will also benefit.

INSULATION

It's an interesting fact that most homes, built in the days when energy was plentiful and cheap, don't have enough insulation, and some don't have any at all. The expression "better late than never" surely applies here.

No matter where you live, insulation is a hidden but most important part of your house. During the heating season, insulation keeps warmth indoors where it belongs, and your family is comfortable and snug. Insulation is equally important in hot weather, since it helps keep the extreme heat of the sun from penetrating. And, in air-conditioned homes, insulation eases the task of the cooling system.

A properly insulated house costs far less to heat and cool than its noninsulated twin. Less fuel is burned, and at the same time a higher level of comfort is experienced. By the same token, air conditioners that work less use less electricity. It can truthfully be said that insulation pays for itself over and over again.

An insulated home is also a far more pleasant place in which to live. Indoor temperatures can be kept more constant. Inside surfaces of walls, floors, and ceilings, insulated from outdoor extremes, are closer to room air temperature and therefore conducive to comfort and well-being. Annoying drafts are minimized or eliminated, and the whole living area stays comfortable in the coldest, or hottest, weather.

Blanket.

Batt.

Loose fill insulation.

In the heating season alone, adequate insulation in the attic floor generally saves up to 30 percent on fuel bills and can save up to 50 percent. In an air-conditioned home, summer savings are comparable.

The most common kinds of insulation for the home are mineral fiber, cellulose fiber, plastic foam, and aluminum foil sheets. These types can be divided into categories according to how they are installed.

Mineral fiber insulation is purchased in batts or blankets and is the most widely used type. Mineral fiber, whether fiberglass or rock wool, is used to insulate unfinished attic floors, attic rafters, and the underside of floors. Batts come precut in widths of either 15 or 23 inches and in lengths of 4 or 8 feet. Blankets are purchased in the same widths and are cut to the desired length. All mineral fiber insulation can be bought with or without a vapor barrier backing and is fire- and moisture-resistant. Installation of this type is very easy.

Loose fill insulation comes in glass fiber, rock wool, cellulose fiber, vermiculite, and perlite. Basically, this type is used only for unfinished attic floors and is best suited for areas that are irregular or have many obstructions. If a vapor barrier is needed, it must be bought and installed separately with this type. Cellulose fiber is chemically treated to be fire- and moisture-resistant but has not yet been proven to be heat-resistant. This means that the insulation could break down in a hot attic. Check to be sure that bags indicate that the material meets federal specifications. Because this type of insulation is simply poured into place, installation is no problem.

Glass fiber, rock wool, and cellulose fiber can also be blown into place. Generally used for attic floors and finished frame walls, this type has the same physical properties as poured-in loose fill. Because it consists of smaller tufts, cellulose fiber gets into small nooks and corners more consistently than rock wool or glass fiber when blown into closed spaces such as walls or joist spaces. Professional installation is required with this insulation.

Ureaformaldehyde can also be used for unfinished attic floors or finished frame walls. Foamed in place, it may have higher insulating value than blown-in materials, but it is more expensive. The quality of application to date has been very inconsistent, so choose a qualified contractor who will guarantee his work.

Regardless of the type of material from which insulation is manufactured or the physical form in which it is applied to the house, the principle remains the same. Between the fibers are tiny air spaces. There are untold numbers of these in each piece of insulation, and each one is a tiny insulator in its own right. The cumulative effect is what does the job. By creating an extremely effective barrier to the passage of heat, the insulation isolates the house from exterior weather influences.

Your money's worth in insulation is mea-

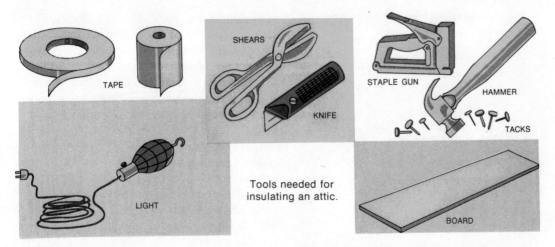

Tools needed for insulating an attic.

sured in R-Value. R-Value is a number that tells how much resistance the insulation presents to heat flowing through it. The higher the R-Value, the better the insulation. One brand of insulation might be slightly thicker or thinner than another, but if they're marked with the same R-Value they'll resist heat flow equally well. If you have a choice of insulating materials, simply price the same R-Value for both and get the better buy. Pay more only for more R-Value. The R-Value is marked on the outside of the package.

Insulating the attic floor, where savings generally will be greatest, usually can be done by the homeowner himself. The amount of insulation needed depends entirely upon how much insulation, if any, is

Measure present insulation in floor.

already there. To find out, go up into the attic and measure the depth with a tape measure or yardstick.

If there is 6 inches or more, no additional insulation is needed. Insulation with an R-Value of R-11 should be used in attics with between 2 and 6 inches of insulation already in place. If there is no insulation at all present, new insulation should have an R-Value of R-22. If you can't get into your attic or don't want to do the work yourself, call a reputable contractor and get an estimate for the needed R-Value. These amounts will make certain that your home meets current Federal Housing Administration standards for new houses.

Amounts greater than these may be necessary if your climate is substantially colder or warmer than average or a high amount of attic insulation will have to partially compensate for poorly insulated walls.

A minimum of tools and experience are needed to insulate an attic properly. Besides the insulation, the materials needed are: tape (2 inches wide), staple gun or hammer and tacks, heavy-duty shears or knife to cut insulation, and temporary lighting and flooring.

Some simple safety steps should be taken when working in the attic with insulation of any type. Provide good lighting (it's dark up

Use board to form walkway on joists.

Watch out for nails!

What the well-dressed insulator will wear: gloves, breathing mask, long-sleeved clothing.

resulting water vapor can wet the insulation, robbing it of its insulating qualities. Excessive moisture can also cause rotting in the wood used to build the house. Added ventilation will remove water vapor before it gets a chance to condense and will also increase summer comfort by cooling your attic.

If you are installing batt or blanket insulation, buy the type with the vapor barrier attached (unless you are adding more insulation on top of existing insulation, in which case no vapor barrier should be used). Install it with the vapor barrier side toward the living space.

For loose fill insulation, lay down polyethylene sheets between the joists before pouring in, or blowing in, the insulation.

The actual job of insulating an attic is quite simple. If batts or blankets with vapor barrier attached are used, merely lay the insulation between joists or trusses. Loose fill insulation is poured between the joists up to the top of the joists. Use a rake or board to level it. Fill all the nooks and crannies, but don't cover recessed light fixtures or exhaust fans. The National Electrical Code requires that insulation be kept at least 3 inches away from light fixtures.

Extra precautions must be taken not to cover any vents that would block the flow of air into the attic. The space between the chimney and the wood framing should be filled with noncombustible material, preferably unfaced batts or blankets.

While insulating the attic, it's a good idea to check for roof leaks by looking for water stains or marks. If you find leakage, make repairs before you insulate. Wet insulation is ineffective and can damage the structure of the home.

Insulating a finished or partially finished attic is a little harder because some parts are inaccessible. A contractor can do a complete job, and in some cases this is the best course. If you can get into the unfin-

there!). Lay boards or plywood sheets down over the tops of the joists or trusses to form a walkway. Be careful of roofing nails protruding through the roof sheathing. If you use glass fiber or mineral wool, wear gloves, a breathing mask, and long-sleeved clothing. Because most insulation comes wrapped in a compressed state, it should be kept wrapped until ready for use.

A vapor barrier is usually necessary when insulation is installed. This is a material that will block moisture and not absorb it. If warm, moist air from inside the house is allowed to pass through the wall covering and meet the cool dry air from outside, the

Polyethylene sheet as vapor barrier.

Lay batts or blankets in place.

Pour in loose fill insulation.

Level loose fill insulation.

Do not cover fixtures.

Do not cover vents.

Noncombustible material should be used for insulation around chimneys.

Check for roof leaks.

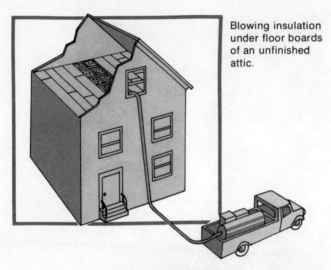

Blowing insulation under floor boards of an unfinished attic.

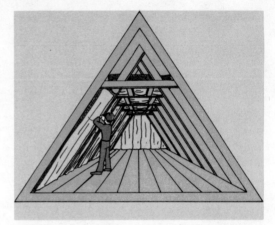

Insulating rafters, end walls, and collar beams.

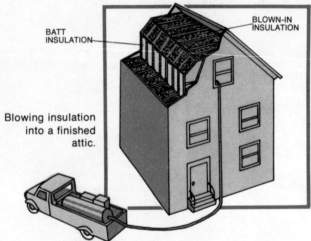

BATT INSULATION

BLOWN-IN INSULATION

Blowing insulation into a finished attic.

ished parts of the attic to do the work, you can do the job yourself.

Insulating an attic that is unfinished but has a floor is usually a job for a contractor. Assuming there is less than 4 inches of insulation under the floor, insulation can be blown under the floor boards. If there is more than 4 inches, the job is not economical.

The do-it-yourselfer can insulate the rafters, end walls, and collar beams of an unfinished, floored attic. This is the best way if you are planning to finish the attic. Batts or blankets are installed between the rafters and collar beams, and between the studs on the end walls. At ceiling height, 2×4 beams must be installed between each roof rafter, if the attic doesn't already have them. This gives a ventilation space above the insulation and forms the roof of the attic. Between the collar beams, add insulation with an R-Value of at least R-22. Rafters and end walls require insulation thick enough to fill up the rafter and stud space. Insulation for the rafters should be R-19, and the end walls should have at least R-11 insulation.

The homeowner with a completely finished attic is more limited as to what he can do himself. Insulating an attic without tearing down the finished walls is almost always a job for a competent contractor. A contractor will blow insulation into the open joist spaces above the attic ceiling, between the rafters, and into the floor of the outer attic space, then install batts in the knee walls. If you want the outer attic spaces heated for storage or any other purpose, have the contractor install batts between the outer attic rafters instead of insulating the outer floors and knee walls. Insulating this type of attic is not worth considering unless there is less than 4 inches of insulation already installed.

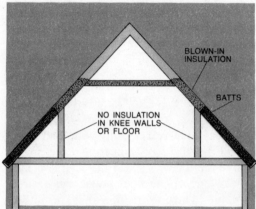

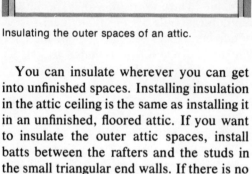

Insulating the outer spaces of an attic.

Installing insulation in the attic ceiling.

You can insulate wherever you can get into unfinished spaces. Installing insulation in the attic ceiling is the same as installing it in an unfinished, floored attic. If you want to insulate the outer attic spaces, install batts between the rafters and the studs in the small triangular end walls. If there is no existing insulation, use R-22 for the ceiling and R-11 for the end walls.

The next step toward easing your energy bills and adding to the comfort of your home is to insulate the walls. This depends on what type of walls you have and how much, if any, insulation is already there.

To find out what's inside the wall, turn off the principal electric switch or a circuit breaker or fuse for a convenient outlet or switch box on an outside wall. Remove the cover plate and the electrical box (usually nailed to a framing member) to get a look inside the wall cavity. You'll be able to see or feel any insulation that's in the wall stud cavity space. If you are in doubt as to the amount of insulation, or whether it will be adequate, your best bet is to call an insulation contractor.

Most frame houses have a wood structure—usually 2×4s—even though they may have brick or stone on the outside. If you have this type of walls, you should consider insulating them if they are not already insulated. A contractor can fill them with insulation and cut energy waste by about two-thirds. This job is not for the do-it-yourselfer.

The contractor will measure the area you want insulated to determine how much material he will need and to estimate the cost. To install the insulation, the contractor must be able to get at all the spaces in the wall. For each space, he must drill a hole, usually in the outside wall, after removing the finish layer (usually clapboard or shingle). This amounts to a lot of holes, but once the job is complete, a good contractor will leave no traces behind.

If you have brick veneer on the outside, the procedure is much the same, except

Check for
insulation in walls.

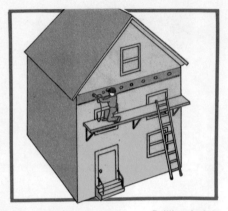

Drilling holes
into the
outside wall.

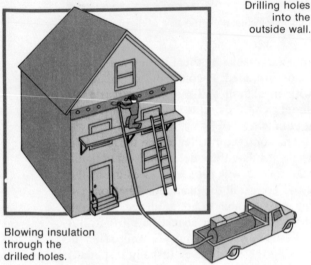

Blowing insulation
through the
drilled holes.

add an R-Value of 8 for rock wool, 10 for cellulose fiber, or 11.5 for ureaformalde-hyde in a standard wood-frame wall. You should agree with the contractor on what the R-Value is before the job begins. Next, check a bag of the type of insulation he intends to use (there will only be bags of mineral fiber or cellulose fiber—there's no good way to check quantity with foam). On it will be a table indicating how many square feet of wall space that bag is meant to fill while giving your house the desired R-Value. The information may be in different forms (number of square feet per bag or number of bags per 1,000 square feet), so you may have to do some simple arithmetic to interpret the number correctly. Knowing this and the area of the walls to be insulated, you should be able to figure out about how many bags should be installed to give you the desired R-Value.

This number should be agreed on between you and the contractor before the job is begun. While the job is in progress be sure the correct amount is being used. There's nothing wrong with having the contractor save the empty bags so you can count them. Four or five bags more or less than the amount you agreed on is an acceptable difference from the estimate.

Some houses have structural brick or masonry walls without a wooden frame behind. Insulating this type of wall is more complicated than frame walls but may be worthwhile if there is no insulation already there. Call a contractor to get an estimate and find out what's involved.

If you are adding a room or have unfinished walls, the job of insulating them is relatively simple. If stud spacing is standard (16 inches, center to center), push blankets or batts into the space between the studs until they touch the sheathing or siding. Be sure to place them so that the vapor barrier faces inward. Fit flanges tightly against the sides of the studs and begin sta-

that it may be cheaper to do the job from the inside.

Once the holes have been made in the walls, the contractor will blow the insulation material under air pressure through a big flexible hose into the area to be filled. If the contractor uses foam-type insulation, he'll pump the foam into the wall spaces with a flexible hose and an applicator. With either method, each space will be completely filled, and the siding replaced.

Before you sign an agreement with the contractor, define what you're buying and make sure it's spelled out in the contract. Insulation material properly installed will pling at the top with a heavy-duty stapler. Space staples about 6 to 12 inches apart. To fill a stud space that is less than standard, cut the insulation lengthwise about an inch wider than the space and then staple normally.

To help prevent condensation in insulated walls, seal any openings that could afford a path to moisture, especially around the window and door frames. Painting the interior walls with a low-permeability paint, such as high-gloss enamel, will also help in this respect. Discuss this matter with a paint dealer before purchasing paint.

If you live in a climate where your heating bills are big enough to be a major hassle, it's a good idea to insulate the underside of your house. It won't save much on air conditioning, but it certainly will save on heating expenses.

If your house (or part of it) sits on top of a crawl space that can be tightly sealed off from the outside air in the winter, the cheapest and best place to insulate is around the outside walls and on the ground inside the space. This should be considered only if there is no existing insulation and if the crawl space is big enough to allow plenty of room to do the work.

First cover the earth inside the crawl space with a layer of 6-mil polyethylene plastic, sealing it to the walls and at seams with 2-inch-wide duct tape or masking tape.

Install batt or blanket insulation (R-11) around the walls of the crawl space, fastening it to the sills by nailing through $\frac{1}{4} \times 1\frac{1}{2}$-inch strips of lattice. Cut the insulation long enough to allow it to overlap the floor by 2 feet. When all the insulation is in place, secure it by laying 2×4s along the wall-floor bend. Force insulation against the header joists and the end joists to insure a good weather seal.

Even with a plastic vapor barrier on the floor, the air in the crawl space will be too damp if fresh air doesn't get in. This will mean that the new insulation will be wet and won't keep the house as warm. It will also mean that wooden framing members will be wet, and they'll rot. Proper ventilation will prevent both of these problems.

If the crawl space is part of the forced-air heating system, seal it as tightly as possible — the air moving through it from the furnace is enough ventilation in winter. If the crawl space has vents, keep them shut in winter, open in summer. If there are no vents, run the blower on the furnace three or four times during the summer to keep the air in the crawl space from getting too damp, preventing wetting the insulation.

All other crawl spaces should have vents that can be opened in summer to clear out the damp air and closed very tightly in winter to make the most of your new insulation. A word of caution: Your furnace may

Insulating a new wall.

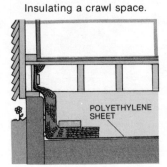

Insulating a crawl space.

POLYETHYLENE SHEET

Seal all openings around windows and door frames.

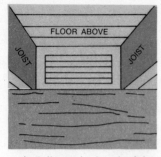

Install vent in header joist.

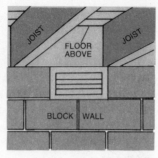

Install vent in block wall.

Staple chicken wire below joists.

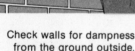

Slide batts or blankets on top of the wire.

Check walls for dampness from the ground outside.

Seal cracks with epoxy patching compound.

get its combustion air from the crawl space. If so, some of the vents should be left open year-round. Check with your fuel oil dealer or gas utility if you are not sure.

Insulating crawl spaces should not be done if you live in Alaska, Minnesota, or northern Maine. The extreme frost penetration in these areas can cause heaving of the foundation if the insulation method described here is used. Residents of these areas should contact local building code officials or government agencies for advice.

Insulating the floor of your house is a good idea if you have a crawl space that you can't seal off in winter, or if you have a garage, porch, or other cold unheated space with heated rooms above it. Install batts or blankets, preferably with foil facing, of R-11 rating between the floor joists. Staple wire mesh or chicken wire to the bottom of the joists, and slide the batts or blankets in on top of the wire, leaving an air space between the vapor barrier and the floor.

Check your floor joist spacing—this method will work best with standard 16- or 24-inch joist spacing. If you have irregular spacing there will be more cutting and fitting and some waste of material.

If you have a basement that you use as a living or work space and that has air outlets, radiators, or baseboard units to heat it, you may find that it will pay to add a layer of insulation to the inside of the wall. You only need to insulate the parts of the walls that are above the ground down to about 2 feet below ground level.

Before insulating, check to see whether moisture is coming through the walls from the ground outside. If it is and your walls are damp, eliminate the cause of dampness to prevent the insulation you're about to install from becoming wet and ineffective.

If the dampness is caused by water seeping through cracks in the foundation walls, seal these cracks with an epoxy patching compound, available at most hardware stores. Follow manufacturer's directions for application. If seepage covers a large area, it may indicate a more serious problem of excessive water pressure against the outside of the foundation. The solution here may involve digging down outside the foundation and applying bituminous coatings to the outside of the walls, and laying drain tiles to carry ground water to a drywell or other location away from the house. It's hard labor that you will probably want to leave to an experienced contractor.

Install a framework of 2×3 studs along the walls to be insulated. The bottom plate of the frame should be nailed to the floor with concrete nails, and the top plate nailed to the joists above. Studs should be placed 16 or 24 inches apart between the top and bottom plates.

Batt or blanket insulation rated R-7 should be cut into sections long enough to extend from the top plate to about 2 feet below the ground line. Staple the sections into place between the studs, with the vapor barrier toward the living space. Only in very cold northern climates will there be added benefits by installing the insulation the full height of the wall.

To finish the basement, install wallboard or paneling over the new insulation and furring. Add molding at the top plate and baseboard at the bottom for a basement that's fit for a king—a comfortable king at that!

As in insulating a crawl space, residents of Alaska, Minnesota, and northern Maine should check local practices before insulating basement walls.

In recent years the family of insulation products has grown to include merchandise for such specialized requirements as sound control, window sealing, and insulating suspended ceilings. Insulation can now be purchased for any purpose, leaving the homeowner no excuse for not wrapping his home with a warm blanket of insulation and saving on fuel bills at the same time.

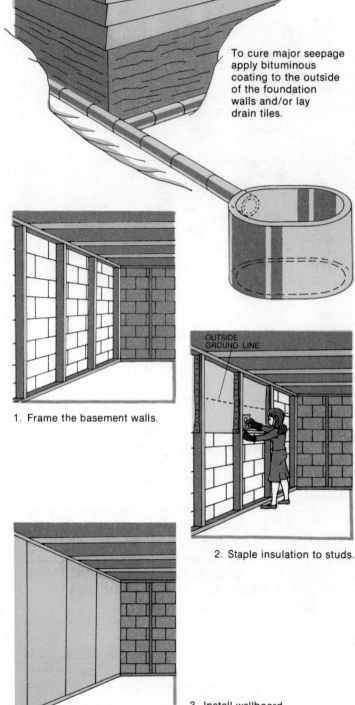

To cure major seepage apply bituminous coating to the outside of the foundation walls and/or lay drain tiles.

1. Frame the basement walls.

OUTSIDE GROUND LINE

2. Staple insulation to studs.

3. Install wallboard over framing.

Calk around windows.

Calk around faucets.

Calk around chimney.

Calk between house and porch.

WEATHERSTRIPPING AND CALKING

In a well-insulated house the largest source of heat loss is air leaks, especially around windows and doors. Good weatherstripping and calking of exterior window and door frames will not only reduce the heat loss in winter and heat gain in summer, but will reduce uncomfortable drafts as well.

Weatherstripping and calking a home are generally worthwhile and economical projects in all climates. The average homeowner can seal his home against the elements for a minimal cost and almost without working up a sweat. Materials are available at most hardware stores.

Calking should be applied wherever two different materials or parts of the house meet. The best way to approach this job is to load up the calking gun and make a thorough examination of the outside of the house, looking for any areas where outside air could leak in.

Common problem areas are around windows and doors, where water faucets, pipes, or wires penetrate the outside house surface, around the chimney, and between the main body of the house and porches.

Calking compound is available in a variety of types and prices to fit anyone's budget. Decide on the type best suited for your needs and the easiest to work with.

Oil- or resin-base calk is readily available and will bond to most surfaces, including wood, masonry, and metal. This type is not the most durable, but it costs the least.

Latex, butyl, or polyvinyl-based calk is also readily available and will bond to most surfaces. It is more durable but more expensive than oil- or resin-based calk.

Elastomeric calks are the most durable and also the most expensive. These include silicones, polysulfides, and polyurethanes. The instructions provided on the labels should be followed.

To fill extra-wide cracks or as a backup for elastomeric calks, use oakum, calking cotton, sponge rubber, or glass fiber.

Lead-based calk is not recommended, because it is toxic. Many states prohibit its use.

Calking a house usually requires the use of a ladder to do the job right. Be sure you use it safely. Carry the calking gun in a sling

Carry calking gun in a sling when climbing (left) and don't overreach (right).

so that you can use both hands climbing the ladder, and don't try to reach for that extra little bit — get down and move the ladder.

Estimating the number of cartridges of calking compound required is difficult, since the number will vary greatly with the size of the cracks to be filled. If possible, it's best to start with a half dozen cartridges and then purchase more as the job continues and you need more.

Before applying calking compound, clean the area to be sealed of paint build-up, dirt, or deteriorated calk, using solvent and a putty knife or other scraping tool.

Drawing a good bead of calk with the gun will take a little practice. First attempts may be a bit messy, but don't get discouraged. Make sure the bead overlaps both sides for a tight seal. Sometimes a wide bead is necessary to do the job right.

Fill extra-wide cracks like those at the sills (where the house meets the foundation) with oakum, glass fiber insulation strips, or similar material, then finish the job with calk.

Calking compound also comes in rope form. This type is forced into cracks with the fingers and is especially good for extra long cracks.

Weatherstripping is another project the homeowner can do to keep the winter chill from entering his domain and to ease high energy costs. A minimum of tools, skills, and cash is required to properly seal doors and windows in a home.

Three types of weatherstripping are commonly used to seal windows. All are readily available at hardware stores or building supply outlets.

Thin spring metal is installed in the channel of a window so that it is virtually invisible when installed. Although somewhat difficult to install, it is very durable.

Rolled vinyl weatherstripping is available with or without a metal backing. It is visible when installed. This type is durable and easy to install.

Foam rubber with adhesive backing is the easiest of all to install, but it breaks down and wears rather quickly. It is not as effective a sealer as metal strips or rolled vinyl and should never be used where friction occurs.

Weatherstripping is purchased either by the running foot or in kit form for each window. In either case, measurements of all windows must be taken to find the total length of weatherstripping needed for the job. Measure the total distance around the

Various kinds of weatherstripping.

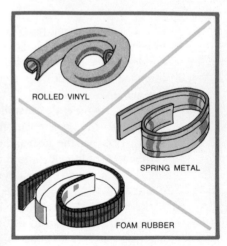

ROLLED VINYL

SPRING METAL

FOAM RUBBER

Clean area before calking.

Fill wide cracks before calking.

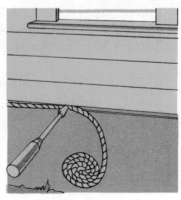

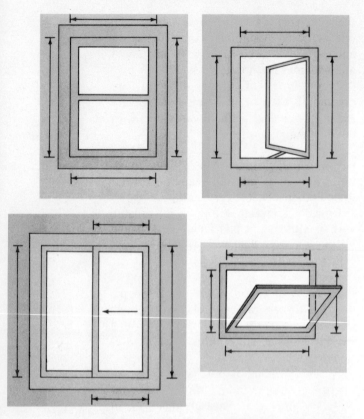

Measuring windows for weatherstripping: double-hung window (top left), casement window (top right), hopper- or awning window (above right), sliding window (above left).

window to the upper sash bottom rail. Countersink the nails slightly so they won't catch on the lower sash top rail.

Nail vinyl strips on double-hung windows so that when the window closes the vinyl will seal any possible air leaks. A sliding window is much the same and can be treated as a double-hung window turned on its side. Casement and tilting windows should be weatherstripped with the vinyl nailed to the window casing so that, as the window shuts, it compresses the roll.

Install adhesive-backed foam, on all types of windows, only where there is no friction. On double-hung windows, this is only on the bottom and top rails. Other

1. Installing spring metal in side channels.

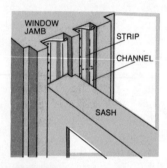

2. Installing spring metal on top and bottom of sash.

3. Installing spring metal between sash.

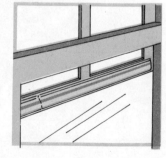

edges of the moving parts of each window to be sealed. Be sure to allow for waste. If a window kit is purchased, be sure the kit is intended for the correct type and size of the window.

Thin spring metal is installed by moving the sash to the open position and sliding a strip in between the sash and the channel. It is then tacked in place into the window casing. Do not cover the pulleys in the upper channel.

Strips should also be installed the full width of the sash on the bottom of the lower sash bottom rail and the top of the upper sash top rail.

Then attach a strip the full width of the

types of windows can use foam strips in other places.

You can weatherstrip your doors even if you're not an experienced handyman. There are several types of weatherstripping for doors, each with its own level of effectiveness. Select the type best suited for your needs.

Foam rubber with either an adhesive or a wood backing can be purchased for the sides and top of a door. Both types are installed on the door jamb to prevent air leaks when the door is closed. They are easy to install, but not very durable.

Rolled vinyl with an aluminum backing is installed much the same as foam to reduce drafts. It is also very easy to install and is much more durable than foam.

The third type of weatherstripping designed for use on the sides and top of a door is spring metal. This is the best type for do-it-yourselfers to use when sealing doors. It is easy to install and extremely durable. After installation in the door jamb, a screwdriver should be used to lift the outer edge for a positive seal.

Accomplished handymen and carpenters can install fitted interlocking channels, the best weather seal available for doors. This technique for sealing doors uses two metal channels, called J-Strips, that interlock when the door is closed, all but eliminating air leaks around the door.

Door sweeps that fit either on the outside or inside of the door are easy to install and are useful for flat thresholds. A drawback is that the sweep will drag on the carpet or rug when the door is opened or closed. Check the supplied instructions for proper installation.

If you feel courageous enough to remove the door, door shoes can be installed. These are useful for wooden thresholds that are not worn, and they are very durable. Remove the door by knocking out the hinge pins with a hammer and screwdriver. If the

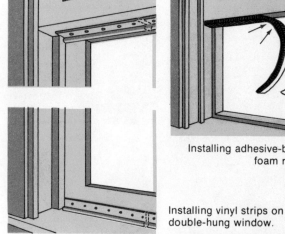

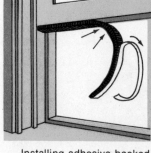

Installing adhesive-backed foam rubber.

Installing vinyl strips on double-hung window.

Installing foam rubber weatherstripping on door jamb (right)

Installing rolled vinyl weatherstripping on door (below).

Installing interlocking channels on a door (below right).

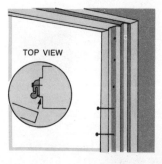

Door sweeps, outside or inside, are easy to install.

1. Knock out hinge pins.

2. Unscrew hinges.

3. Plane bottom of door.

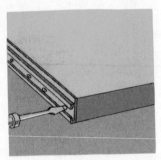

4. Screw on door shoe.

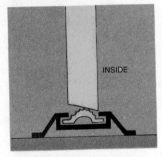

INSIDE

Installing a vinyl threshold
after having removed door.

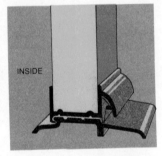

INSIDE

An interlocking threshold is
a very good weather seal.

pins are jammed and can't be removed, unscrew the hinges from the door jamb to take off the door. The shoe is installed by removing a small amount of wood from the bottom of the door with a plane, then screwing the shoe into place.

A vinyl bulb threshold to seal the bottom of the door also requires the removal of the door. If there is no threshold, or the wooden one is worn, this is the best kind to use. A vinyl bulb, similar to the door shoe, is installed on the threshold, and the bottom of the door is beveled with a plane to seal against the vinyl with the door shut. The vinyl will eventually wear out but can be replaced.

An interlocking threshold much like the metal channels for the sides and top of a door can be purchased. Although this type is an exceptionally good weather seal, it is very difficult to install, and the job should be done only by a skilled carpenter.

STORM SASH

Windows and doors can be big energy wasters. This is because doors and windows that open have cracks all around them allowing air to pass through the joints and around window and door frames if they are not tightly sealed. Another reason is that glass itself is a highly heat-conductive material.

Storm windows and doors cut heat loss (or heat gain) at these points about in half. Insulating glass (two panes of glass sealed together at the edges) has approximately the same effect. Triple glazing (insulating glass plus a storm window) is even more effective and often is used in extremely cold climates.

According to the National Bureau of Standards, an investment in storm windows will pay for itself in a decade, including interest costs at 6 percent, and thereafter return an annual dividend of 13 percent. This is based on a climate where winter temperatures are similar to those of Washington, D.C. In regions of the country where snow lies on the ground all winter, payback will occur in less than 7 years, the NBS says. And with fuel costs rising rapidly, this time period will shrink considerably.

There are basically three kinds of storm windows, each providing about the same effectiveness. The more expensive ones are more attractive and convenient, but not more effective.

Plastic sheeting, available in hardware stores, makes effective storm sash. At a cost of only about 50 cents per window, no home located in a cold region should go without at least this type of storm sash. Because of the low price, this type is also ideal for people who rent homes.

Measure the width of your larger windows to determine the width of the plastic rolls to buy. Measure the length of your windows to see how many linear feet and therefore how many rolls or the kit size you need to buy.

Attach to the inside or outside of the frame so that the plastic will block airflow that leaks around the movable parts of the window. If you attach the plastic to the outside, use $1/4 \times 1 1/4$-inch wood slats and tacks around the edges. If you decide to attach it to the inside, masking tape will work.

Inside installation is easier and provides greater protection to the plastic. Outside installation is more difficult, especially on a two-story house, and the plastic is more likely to be damaged by the elements.

Be sure to install tightly and securely, and remove all excess. Besides looking better, a clean installation will make the plastic less susceptible to deterioration during the course of the winter.

Storm window suppliers will build single-pane aluminum storm windows to your measurements that you can install yourself. Cost is about $10 to $20 per window. This type of storm sash is taken down at the end of winter.

Determine how you want the windows to fit in the frame. Your measurements will be the outside measurements of the storm window. Be as accurate as possible, then allow $1/8$ inch along each edge for clearance. You'll be responsible for any errors in measurement, so do a good job.

When the windows are delivered, check the actual size against your order. A poor window fit will mean possible air leakage.

Install the windows and fix in place with movable clips so that you can take them down easily. The side of the aluminum frame that touches the window frame should have a permanently installed weatherstrip or gasket to seal the crack between the window and the single-pane storm window frames.

Single-pane storm windows built to your specification.

Triple-track combination storm window.

Insulating glass prevents heat loss or gain (right).

Plastic sheeting attached to the outside of the window (center).

Plastic sheeting attached to the inside of the window (far right).

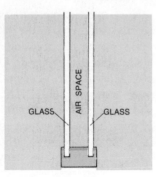

Drill drainage holes, if your units don't have them already.

Single-pane storm windows aren't as expensive as the double-track or triple-track combination windows. The disadvantage of the single-pane windows is that they can't be opened easily once they are installed.

A mill finish (plain aluminum) will oxidize quickly and degrade appearance. Windows with an anodized or baked enamel finish look better.

Triple-track combination (windows and screen) storm windows are designed for installation over double-hung windows only. They cost about $30 to $45 per window. They are permanently installed and can be opened any time with a screen slid into place for ventilation.

Double-track combination units are also

Corner joints should be strong and airtight.

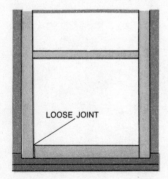

LOOSE JOINT

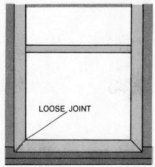

LOOSE JOINT

available at a lower cost. Both kinds are sold almost everywhere, and can be bought with or without the cost of installation.

You can save a few dollars (10 to 15 percent) by installing the windows yourself, but in most cases it is better to have the supplier install the windows for you, even though it costs a bit more.

When the windows are installed, make sure that both the window sashes and screen sash move smoothly and seal tightly when closed. Poor installation can cause misalignment.

Be sure there is a tightly calked seal around the edge of the storm window. Leaks can hurt the performance of storm windows considerably.

Most combination units come with two or three small holes (or other types of vents) drilled through the frame where it meets the window sill. This is to keep winter condensation from collecting on the sill and causing rot. Keep these holes clear, or drill them yourself if your units don't already have them.

The quality of construction affects the strength and performance of storm windows. Corners are a good place to check construction. They should be strong and airtight. Normally, overlapped corner joints are better than mitered. If you can see through the joints, they will leak air.

Storm windows are supposed to reduce air leakage around windows. The depth of the metal grooves (sash tracks) at the sides of the window and the weatherstripping quality make a big difference in how well storm windows can do this. Compare several types before deciding.

Combination (windows and screen) storm doors are designed for installation over exterior doors. They are sold just about everywhere, with or without the cost of installation. In most cases, it is easier to have the supplier install the doors.

Before the installer leaves, be sure the

doors operate smoothly and close tightly. Check for cracks around the jamb, and make sure the seal is as airtight as possible. Also, remove and replace the exchangeable panels (window and screen) to make sure they fit properly and with a weathertight seal.

The same rules apply to judging the quality of storm doors as apply to storm windows. Corner joints, weatherstripping, and hardware quality should be checked.

Storm doors of wood or steel can also be purchased within the same price range as the aluminum variety. They have the same quality differences and should be similarly evaluated. The choice between doors of similar quality but different materials is primarily up to your own taste.

EQUIPMENT LOCATION

Often, the location of heating and cooling equipment is only casually considered when it is being installed, and then "out of sight, out of mind" may be the deciding factor. This can cause problems. In addition to forcing the units to work overtime to do their job, poor circulation of heated (or cooled) air and higher fuel bills will be the consequence.

Even though the advent of forced-air systems allowed the positioning of the furnace and blower at almost any location, the most efficient place remains near the center of the house. This location enables the blower to distribute heated air through the network of ducts more evenly, reducing hot spots or cold spots. Keep this in mind when building a home or adding a new room.

Air conditioners can also be installed in places that are not advantageous to maximum efficiency. The part of the conditioner that is on the outside of the house should not be in direct sunlight all day. Heat from the sun will overload the unit's cooling ca-

Good location for condenser of air conditioner.

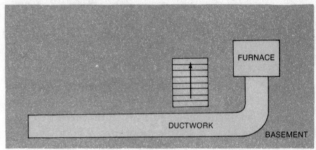

Poor furnace location.

Good furnace location.

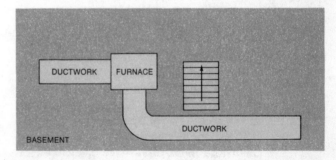

pacity, causing it to work harder than necessary to cool the house. If shade from buildings, trees, etc., is not available, build a small awning to shade the condenser unit from the sun. The condenser should not be placed where tall grass, dirt, or leaves can collect on the coils or obstruct air flow, reducing the air conditioner's ability to do its job.

If you've ever waited for what seemed like hours for hot water to come out of the shower or bathroom faucet, you already know the benefits of having a centrally located hot-water heater.

OPERATING ECONOMY

A periodic checkup and maintenance of heating and cooling equipment can reduce fuel consumption by about 10 percent. Finding a good heating/cooling specialist and sticking with him is a good way to ensure that your equipment stays in top fuel-saving condition.

Check out the people you contact with the Better Business Bureau and other homeowners in your area. Once you're confident you're in touch with a reputable outfit, a service contract is the best arrangement to make. For an annual fee, this provides a periodic tune-up of your heating/cooling system and insures you against repairs of most components.

There are some service jobs you can do yourself and save even more money. Study any manuals you might have concerning the equipment or have a serviceman show you how to do certain routine maintenance chores before you start tinkering.

An oil-burning furnace should be cleaned and adjusted each year for maximum efficiency. Check for oil leaks in the system, and change the oil and air filters annually.

There are also several tests servicemen can use to check oil furnace efficiency (see CHAPTER 5). If you suspect a problem, call a serviceman immediately.

Coal furnaces should also be serviced at the end of each heating season. Adjust and clean the stoker, clean the burner of all coal, ash, and clinkers, and oil the inside of the coal screw and hopper to prevent rust. Furnaces that use bottled, LP, or natural gas should be attended to every three years.

Valves and nozzles should be cleaned and adjusted for best operation.

Hot-water heating systems should be checked yearly by a serviceman. Once or twice a year open the valve at each radiator to rid the system of trapped air. If you are in doubt as to how to do this, consult your serviceman.

Forced hot-air heating systems have air filters that should be cleaned or replaced every 30 to 60 days during the heating season. Ask your serviceman how to do this, buy a supply of filters, and stick to a schedule. You can save a lot of fuel this way.

The blower fan and all registers should also be cleaned periodically on forced-air systems. Dirt at either of these locations will greatly reduce the unit's capacity.

The best preventive medicine for steam heat systems is to drain a bucket of water from the boiler every three weeks during the heating season. This will keep the sediment off the bottom of the boiler. If the sediment is allowed to remain, it will actually insulate the boiler from the flame in the burner.

In addition to the checks and adjustments a serviceman can do, the filters in a whole-house air conditioner should be replaced often. If the filters are cleaned or replaced every 30 to 60 days you will save far more money in fuel than the cost of the filters.

A water heater is another piece of equipment that should not be overlooked in your maintenance schedule. Every three months,

Replacing central air conditioner filter.

Drain water from the heater tank.

Seal air escape routes between attic and the rest of the house.

drain a bucket of water from the spigot at the bottom of the heater tank. A real energy waster is a water heater that is set too high. If you have a dishwasher, 140 degrees is high enough. If not, 120 degrees is plenty. Depending on the type of fuel used, this simple setback will save $5 to $45 a year.

COMMON SENSE DOLLAR SAVERS

Keep doors and windows firmly shut and locked to cut down heat loss in winter and heat gain in summer. Check your window and door latches to see whether they fit tightly and, if necessary, adjust the latches and plug any air leaks. You don't really need to open windows in winter—you usually get enough fresh air just from normal air leakage even if your house is well calked and weatherstripped.

Seal any openings between the attic and the rest of the house where air might escape, such as spaces around loosely fitting attic stairway doors or pull-down stairways, penetrations of the ceiling for lights or a fan, and vents, pipes, etc. It may not seem like much, but it adds up!

If you can't get inside your crawl space, you can still create some barriers against wind and cold by planting shrubs around the foundation. You can also tar-paper the

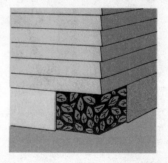

Protect foundation with shrubs (above) or tarpaper (right), if you can't get inside your crawl space to insulate it.

outside walls and rake leaves against the foundation, covering them with a weighted tarpaulin. The same holds true of a basement foundation.

A good way to keep your house cool in the summer is to keep the sun out. Large shade trees on the east and west sides will help tremendously. Awnings and sunshades will also help keep the inside of your home cool. Anything that stops the sun

A good way to keep your house cool is to keep the sun out.

before it gets in through the glass is seven times as good at keeping you cool as blinds and curtains on the inside.

All leaky faucets should be fixed, particularly the hot ones. One leaky faucet can waste up to 6,000 gallons of water a year.

FIX LEAKY FAUCETS:

1. Remove packing nut.

2. Remove stem.

3. Remove old washer.

4. Replace washer.

WASHER

You can also save by turning the hot-water heater down when you'll be away from home for a weekend or more. Always use full loads in the dishwasher and clothes washer, and use warm wash and cold rinse. Take showers—they use less hot water than baths. You should use cold water to run the garbage disposal. In general, every time you use cold water instead of hot, you save.

You can notice a substantial savings in fuel costs by lowering your thermostat. For an investment of about $80 you can install a clock thermostat, which will automatically turn the heat down at night and up in the morning.

If your house was not insulated when it was built, but is now, your furnace may be too big. In general, that means that it is inefficient and would use less fuel if it were smaller. Wait for one of the coldest nights of the year, and set your thermostat at 70 degrees. Once the house temperature reaches 70 degrees, if the furnace burner runs less than 40 minutes during the next hour (time it only when it's running), your furnace is too big. A furnace that is too big turns on and off much more often than it should, and that wastes energy. Depending on the type of fuel burner, a serviceman may be able to cut down the size of your burner without replacing it.

Don't overheat rooms and don't heat or cool rooms you're not using. It's important that no room in your house get more heat than it needs, and that you should be able to turn down the heating or cooling in areas of your home that you don't use. Most heating systems have valves or dampers to regulate the amount of heat room by room. If you have hot spots in your home and can't solve the problem yourself, call a serviceman.

Closing off unused rooms is just as important in saving on air conditioning as it is for heating. Keep lights off during the day—most of the electricity they use makes heat, not light. You can also reduce the load on your air-conditioning system by not running heat-generating appliances like the dishwasher during the hot part of the day.

If you have central air conditioning, you may want to look into the air economizer, a system that turns off the part of the conditioner that uses a lot of electricity and circulates outside air through the house when it's cooler out than it is in. Ask your dealer if he can install one on your central system.

When adding a room, consider adding a room-size heat pump. A heat pump runs on electricity and is just like an air conditioner, except that it can run in reverse. It gets more heat out of a dollar's worth of electricity than the resistance heaters in baseboard units and electric furnaces.

The last energy-saving tip is probably the most obvious, but usually not considered — lighting. Plan your lighting sensibly and reduce lighting where possible, concentrat-

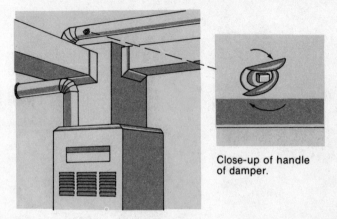

Close-up of handle of damper.

Adjust the heating system to regulate the amount of heat for each room.

ing it in work areas or reading areas where it is really needed. Fluorescent bulbs should be used rather than incandescent. A 25-watt fluorescent bulb gives off as much light as a 100-watt incandescent bulb but costs one-fourth as much to light.

8

Other Comfort Factors

"IT'S NOT THE HEAT, IT'S THE HUMIDITY." How many times have you heard this old saw from some sage trying to explain why you feel like a parboiled dishrag as you perspire your way through an August day? He is right, of course. Humidity and the lack of it play a very important role in your comfort. There may not be much you can do about the outside humidity, short of surrounding yourself with it in the form of a swimming pool or a cool lake, but you can control it in your house—a vital factor in comfort conditioning.

HUMIDIFICATION

As the cool, dry air of winter is heated in your home, it becomes even drier. On a cold day, the air inside a home without proper humidification may actually be twice as dry as hot desert air. Just as with desert travelers, throats become parched and sore. Lung irritations, sinus problems, and colds result. Plants wither, furniture dries up and comes apart at glued joints, and even rugs and draperies become brittle. To add insult to misery, temperatures must be kept high—much higher than the energy-conserving recommended 65 degrees—to provide comfort. By adding moisture to the air in the proper proportions, you can lower the thermostat 10 degrees or more, be perfectly comfortable, and save many dollars as well. For every degree over 70 degrees F. that you heat your house, at least 3 percent more fuel is consumed, so that 10 degrees can mean a 30 percent or greater fuel saving!

In the "good old days," humidification meant putting a tin can filled with water atop the stove or radiator. And it worked. Today, more sophisticated devices are generally employed, but if you live in an old

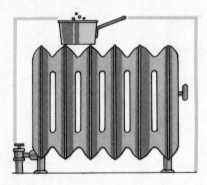

Humidification in the good old times.

house or apartment without proper humid-ification, by all means use the tin-can method. Better an unsightly tin can than unhealthful discomfort.

Most modern warm-air furnaces include some kind of humidifier. If yours does not, it is a relatively simple and inexpensive installation, and one that will quickly pay for itself in reduced fuel bills, not to mention increased comfort. Many such units can also be used in conjunction with other heating systems (hot water, steam).

There are two basic types of humidifiers: evaporator and atomizer. In evaporator types, warm air moving over water in the unit picks up moisture, which is then circulated throughout the house. The simpler types consist of a water-filled pan inside the furnace plenum, but most now include a motor and fan assembly to draw the air through the humidifier and push it back into the ductwork. A supply pipe from the house cold-water plumbing system carries water to the humidifer, and a humidistat can be set to a desired humidity level, which is then automatically maintained.

Atomizer-type humidifiers are placed in the cold-air returns of warm-air furnaces. They break up water into tiny particles that are absorbed by air passing through. Some types can also be placed at a distance from the furnace—in a utility room or cabinet—and rigged to provide access to household air. If properly located, such units can effectively humidify the entire house.

Installation procedures for both types of humidifiers vary greatly, and manufacturer's instructions should be scrupulously followed.

Many warm-air furnaces, particularly earlier or smaller models, are equipped with evaporative-plate humidifiers, which work by capillary action. These are not as efficient as the powered units and are subject to frequent clogging by mineral deposits. If you have such a unit, keep it regularly ser-

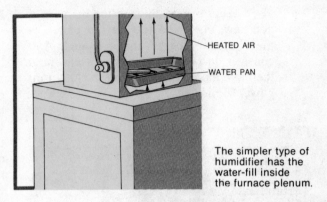

The simpler type of humidifier has the water-fill inside the furnace plenum.

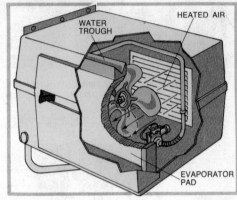

Power humidifier.

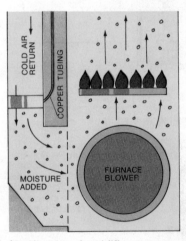

Atomizer-type humidifier.

Evaporative-plate humidifier (pan with plates, one being replaced).

viced according to the service manual (if you have one), and replace the plates as they become clogged and corroded. And consider installing a more efficient (and therefore more economical in the long run) power humidifier.

Sure signs of excess humidity: moisture on walls and windows, sweating pipes and mildew in the basement.

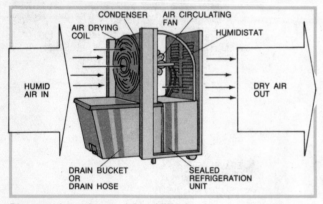

Diagram shows how a dehumidifier works.

DEHUMIDIFICATION

It's a matter of famine or feast—your home's air may need to be humidified, but it may also be too humid. You have "buttoned it up" so securely with vapor barriers that there is no way for inside water vapor to get out. Cooking, bathing, washing, and even breathing by the house occupants cause excessive humidity. Physical discomfort is noticed because the natural rate of evaporation from the skin is slowed down by the ambient humidity. Moisture forms on windows and walls. In the summertime, plumbing pipes sweat, and bread turns moldy. Mildew forms on walls and other surfaces, and paint deteriorates. Don't despair—dehumidify!

A portable dehumidifier is built somewhat like an air conditioner but is designed to dry air rather than cool it. It consists of a refrigerated air-drying coil, a condenser, a fan, and a humidistat, all housed in a cabinet that may be designed as a piece of furniture so that it can fit unobtrusively in any room. The fan draws moisture-laden air over the coil; the cold coil causes the moisture to condense, and it is carried off through a drain or collected in a bucket as the air passes through. The collection bucket must be emptied regularly; if there is a drain hose, it should be connected to a

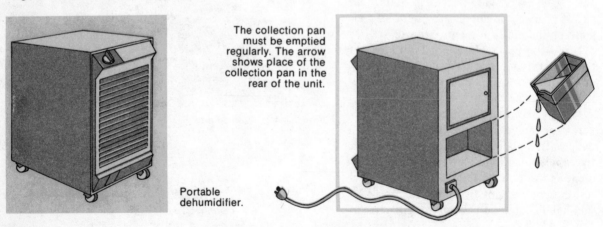

The collection pan must be emptied regularly. The arrow shows place of the collection pan in the rear of the unit.

Portable dehumidifier.

drainage pipe or led to a basement drain or other drain opening.

The minimum water-removal capacity of a dehumidifier in a house or apartment in the "average" temperate summer climate is roughly one pint per day for every hundred square feet of floor space. If the space includes a laundry, bath, or kitchen, figure an additional 50 percent over the minimum. A specially hot and muggy climate, a large and active family, or a house with many doors and windows may double these requirements.

All dehumidifiers are equipped with three-prong plugs for connecting to three-hole, grounded electrical outlets. Such an outlet protects you from shock or burn if the unit malfunctions. This is especially important for a dehumidifier because it may be operated on a damp floor that could conduct electricity, and because it collects water, which could spill and cause an electrical accident. Don't commit the grievous error of snapping off the third prong from the plug so that it fits into a two-hole outlet. Water, metal, and electricity can be a lethal mix. If you have no three-hole grounded outlet, have an electrician convert a two-hole outlet. Three-prong adapters are a poor substitute.

Always read the owner's manual and follow its directions. Place the dehumidifier at

Proper location for a dehumidifier.

Vacuum clean the grilles regularly.

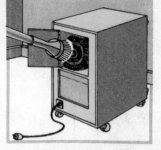

Clean the coils with a soft brush once each season.

least 6 inches from the nearest wall where air can flow freely to and from all sides. Avoid placing it in a room corner or near a large piece of furniture. Close all doors and windows in the area to be dehumidified. For the first few days of operation, set the humidistat (if the unit has one) to "drier" or "extra dry." This aids moisture removal from furnishings as well as room air. After the area has generally dried out, adjust the humidistat to your particular comfort level.

Dehumidifiers need little upkeep, other than regular cleaning. Always disconnect the power cord before cleaning or emptying the collection bucket. Be sure the area, the unit, and you are dry before reconnecting the cord. Regularly dust the grilles or louvers with a soft brush or the dusting attachment of a vacuum cleaner. Every few weeks, wash the inside of the water container with a sponge or soft cloth and a mild

Three-prong plug and three-hole outlet.

detergent to discourage the growth of mold, mildew, or bacteria. On cool days, check the cold coils for frosting. If you find any, turn off the unit until the frost has melted. At least once each season, remove all dust and lint from the coils with a soft brush.

Circulating air through the house by means of an attic fan.

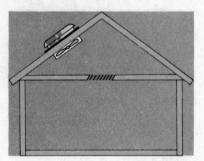

Roof fan.

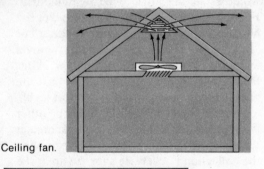

Ceiling fan.

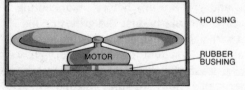

Fan mounting for quiet operation.

HOUSING

MOTOR

RUBBER BUSHING

ATTIC VENTILATION

Circulating air through the house by means of a fan in the attic won't reduce summertime temperatures, but it will give the effect of doing so by helping to evaporate body perspiration. At night, it will replace hot indoor air with cooler, drier outdoor air and, coupled with open windows in strategic locations, will move cool air throughout the entire house. It cannot, however, be used in conjunction with a dehumidifier, which requires a relatively sealed environment to function properly.

There are two basic types of attic fans. One type is mounted in a gable end or in the roof and draws air through a louver in the ceiling below, exhausting it to the outdoors. The rest of the attic is sealed to ensure proper circulation. The other type is mounted in the ceiling, usually in a central location such as a hallway. It draws air up into the attic, where it passes outdoors through louvers, usually located in the gable ends. The louvers must be large enough to permit free passage of the air.

The fan's capacity to do the job is determined by the cubic feet of air it can move per minute. Figure the cubic feet of living space in your house (not including closets, basement, or garage). In most areas of the country, the fan should be able to move approximately two-thirds of this total every minute. In warmer southern areas, it should be able to handle the entire volume once a minute. Check the rating of a fan before you buy.

Quiet operation is an important consideration. Make sure the fan you buy is mounted on rubber bushings or felt sound absorbers or is isolated from its housing by springs. Actual installation will depend on the type and the manufacturer's specific directions, which should be followed to the letter. That way, if something goes wrong, you have only him to blame.

Chapter 8 ● Other Comfort Factors

CONTAMINATED AIR

ELECTRICAL FIELD

POSITIVE-CHARGED AIR

NEGATIVE PLATES

CLEANED AIR

Electronic
air cleaning
(schematic).

ELECTRONIC AIR CLEANING

Even in the cleanest of homes, the air is filled with billions of undesirable particles, most of them so tiny that they are invisible to the human eye. Outdoor air continually enters the home, bringing with it airborne soil particles, particulate wastes (industrial wastes, automobile and airplane exhaust), pollen, and mold spores. Inside the house, dust and other particles are generated from mattresses, pillows, blankets, carpets, fabrics, food such as flour, cooking smoke and grease, animals, and tobacco smoke.

Put them all together and they spell misery, particularly for persons who are especially sensitive to such irritants as dust, pollen, and cigarette smoke. They also cause discoloration and staining of paint and wallpaper and leave greasy deposits on glass, windows, and mirrors.

The filter in a warm-air furnace will remove some of these contaminants. But if you live in an area where air pollution is a serious problem, or if members of your family are especially susceptible to respiratory problems, an electronic air cleaner can be installed as part of the air system of your total home comfort conditioning. Such a unit removes the contaminant particles by electrostatic precipitation—the same principle used at large industrial stacks as required by many local clean-air ordinances.

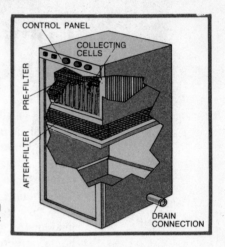

CONTROL PANEL

COLLECTING CELLS

PRE-FILTER

AFTER-FILTER

DRAIN CONNECTION

Self-contained
electrostatic
air cleaner.

The air particles are passed through a powerful electrical field, where they are positively charged. They then pass through a series of negatively charged plates, where they are trapped until they are purified of contaminants. The air is then recirculated.

Electronic air cleaners are available either as self-contained units, which can be placed wherever they are most needed, or as units designed for installation in the ductwork of a central system. Once again, the actual installation will depend on the type you choose, and manufacturer's directions must be followed.

Maintenance is simple. Usually, all you need do is clean the collector plates at intervals as recommended by the manufacturer. In some units, this can be done without even having to remove the plates.

9

Comfort Quotient for Home Buyers

YOU'VE HEARD it said many times: "Buying a home is the biggest financial investment of your lifetime." For most families, that is true. So before you invest, you will want to know what you are getting for that hard-earned 30 years of payments. You certainly don't want to move into that brand-spanking new ranch, or golden oldie Victorian gingerbread fantasy, or that genuine George-Washington-slept-here colonial, and then turn blue from nose to toes with the first chill night because the heating system is inadequate, incompetent, or nonexistent. When you are shopping for a home, structural soundness is a most important consideration; the heating system is not far behind.

THE NEW HOUSE

If you are having a house built, you have the luxury of time to consider what type of heating system will best suit your needs and what type of fuel will be most plentiful and most economical (although there may be some long-range international political prognostications and not a little guesswork involved in making the latter choice). Study CHAPTERS 1 and 2; then, armed with this knowledge, get at least three estimates from reputable heating contractors, making sure that they understand exactly what you want. Get everything in writing before signing on the dotted line with the one you finally select. Insist on quality equipment, and see that you get it.

Central air conditioning is most easily and economically installed when the house is being built, so if that figures in your plans, now is the time to do it. Even if, for financial reasons, the central air conditioning must wait awhile, it will be relatively inexpensive at this stage to provide ductwork for future installation.

If you are thinking of buying a new house that is already built or in which the heating system is already installed, make sure that there are heat outlets in all rooms (except the attic and basement). Many building codes require this, but check it anyway.

Warm-air furnaces should also have cold-air returns in all but the smallest rooms. If the house has an attic that may be finished at a later date, are there risers in the walls that can be hooked up simply and inexpensively to the existing furnace? And is the furnace of adequate capacity to handle future as well as present needs? Is the heating plant of first-rate quality—a known brand and not a cheapie Brand X? It may be difficult for you to answer some of these questions. If you have serious doubts, call in a professional engineer for his opinion—it will be money well spent.

If you are looking at the house during cold weather, turn up the thermostat to at least 60 degrees (the builder or real estate broker probably has it set at the minimum of 55 to keep pipes from freezing and to prevent other cold damage). Wait for the furnace to do its work, then check all the rooms to see that they are evenly heated. A particularly cold room may mean only that a damper needs adjustment—or it may mean that the system is inadequate or poorly designed and can't do the job it should.

Check the insulation. Just about every new home will have at least some insulation—but where, how much, and how effective? If the house is in the early building stages, you can insist on having insulation of the proper R-Value (see CHAPTER 7) installed in walls and ceiling or roof. If walls are already enclosed, at least check out the

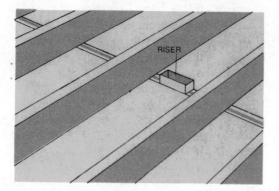

Risers make future heating hookups much easier.

insulation in the attic to make sure it is adequate.

Storm windows or double-glazed windows may come with the house—or they may not. In the latter case, these will probably be among your first acquisitions after, or even before, you move in. You may be strapped for cash, but they should figure into your budget.

THE OLDER HOME

You can't always judge the condition of a furnace or boiler by its age. Some old furnaces, usually coal burners converted to oil or gas, are still cooking away at 40 or even 50 years. Still, it is reasonable to assume that after 12 to 15 years a heating plant becomes weary, and repairs if not replacement are in the offing. If in doubt about the heating system, consult an engineer.

Be suspicious if there are signs of neglect—a sooty combustion chamber, for example, or dirty filters. While these may entail only simple repairs and adjustments, they are an indication of how poorly the system has been cared for.

Check to see if there are heat outlets in all rooms. In older homes, this is not always the case. If there are rooms—a finished attic, for example, or a pantry that has been converted to a small bathroom—how will they be heated? There are many ways, of course (see CHAPTER 4), but they all cost money, which may be in short supply immediately after you buy a house.

Don't be timid about asking the owner of a house you are considering buying to let you see the previous year's heating bills. Take into account whether that winter was unusually cold or uncommonly mild—that will, of course, be reflected in the bills. And even if it's midsummer, don't be afraid to ask that the thermostat be turned up so that you can actually see—and hear, and possibly smell—the system in operation. This is what the professional engineer would do as part of a total house inspection. At a cost of anywhere from $50 to $125, his services may well be worth it if you have questions about a house you are seriously considering buying.

Many older homes are completely uninsulated; others may have only minimal insulation in the attic. Today's fuel costs almost mandate insulation, which will pay for itself in only a few years (see CHAPTER 7). Still, it means another immediate cash outlay, which must figure into your "what-can-I-afford" calculations before you make that hard decision to buy the house.

If there are no storm windows, add more bucks to the comfort cost of buying the house. If there are storms, check them out closely. Old, wood-framed storm windows may become rotten and have to be replaced. Even if they are in good condition, they have to be painted (annually is best) and, unless you have the house sealed for year-round comfort conditioning with summer air conditioning, put up in the fall and taken down in the spring. Double- or triple-track aluminum types mean one less home maintenance chore. But make sure they are in good condition too.

If one or more room air conditioners are included with the house, make sure that they are in working order—even if it is a sub-zero day. And do some quick calculations, using the formulas given in CHAPTER 6, to see if the air conditioner ratings are right for the rooms they are expected to cool. Replacement of a faulty or wrongly sized room air conditioner is only a small factor in the overall price of a house. But why should you pay for something that doesn't work or doesn't work as it should? When you are buying a home, you need to save as many dollars as you can.

Index